Reprint

Northern Parallels
to the Death of Pan

Archer Taylor

Fathom Publishing Company

Introduction and images copyright © 2017 Ann Taylor Schwing. Reproduction or translation of any part of this work beyond that permitted by Section 107 or 108 of the 1976 United States Copyright Act without permission in writing from the copyright owner is unlawful. Requests for permission or further information should be addressed to the publisher.

ISBN: 978-1-888215-73-1
Library of Congress Control Number: 2017959533

First printed in Washington University Studies, Humanistic Series, Volume X (October 1922).

Fathom Publishing Company
PO Box 200448
Anchorage, AK 99520-0448
www.fathompublishing.com
www.archertaylor.com

Archer Taylor

Archer Taylor (center) on an Atlantic cattle boat during a summer trip to Europe during his Swarthmore years.

Archer Taylor (left) with a friend and his sisters.

Introduction to Taylor Reprints

Archer Taylor was born August 1, 1890 and died September 30, 1973. He was called Archer because the family had difficulty agreeing on a name, and his uncle began calling him Sagittarius, symbolized in Greek mythology by the archer—half-man, half-horse in the ninth astrological sign.

Taylor wrote many books and a vast number of articles, some extended studies of the subject at hand and others short notes or queries. He grew up in a world in which academic-minded students learned Latin and Greek in grammar school, and he learned. In the years that followed, he continued to learn. Ultimately he read and spoke thirteen languages, with varying degrees of proficiency to be sure. In high school and early college years at Swarthmore, he worked on a cattle boat to Europe at the start of the summer. Once there, he traveled to the various countries in Europe learning the languages and meeting the people before returning to port to sign on a boat for the trip home. These experiences left him with a love of language and languages (and a life-long dislike for marmalade, pumpernickel and salt pork, the only foods for the crew on the voyage once the fresh things had been eaten). These experiences ended with World War I when he was caught in Europe at the start of the war and had to make his way home. His family sought news of his location and condition in the flyer shown on the next page.

After finishing Swarthmore in three years, Taylor taught and studied, earning his M.A. at the University of Pennsylvania and his PhD at Harvard and publishing his dissertation on the Wolfdietrich epics in 1915. He taught at Washington University in St. Louis starting in 1915, moving to the University of Chicago for the years 1925 into 1939. He ended his teaching

Mr. ARCHER TAYLOR, born August 1st, 1890, West Chester, Pennsylvania, U. S. of America, Father, American born Citizen, Lowndes Taylor, West Chester, Pennsylvania.

Instructor and Assistant Professor for two years at "State College" Pennsylvania.

Specialty, German Language and literature.

He went to Europe in June 1914, to persue special studies toward his Ph. D degree.

He was last heard from by postal mailed Wilhemlshohe, (Bz. Cassel) Germany.

In that postal he announced his intention to go at once to Gottingen.

He gave his address as "Archer Taylor, Dresden, Poste Restante, Germany.

But he has acknowledged no mail so addressed to him.

He has visited Germany several times on summer tours, and is somewhat familiar with the people and their language.

He speaks also a little French.

He is a graduate of Swarthmore College, a Quaker Institution, and also of the University of Pennsylvania.

He was studying at Harvard University for his Doctor's Degree, and went to Germany sssisted by Swarthmore College.

He had sufficient Credits for ordinary purposes and usual expenses in times of peace.

Please assist him in any way possible, also give any information of him to the German Police, and inform the local American Representatives, (Consul &c.)

Also kindly send information pegarding him to his uncle, Ervine D. York, Flushing, New York.

Or to his father,
Lowndes Taylor, West Chester, Pennsylvania,
U. S. of America.

career at the University of California, Berkeley, where he served from 1939 to 1958 and was chairman of the Department of German from 1940 to 1945. Taylor published *The Proverb* in 1931, followed by *Index to the Proverb* in 1934. His *Bibliography of Riddles* was published in 1939, and a number of other riddle books followed. Archer Taylor and Bartlett Jere Whiting published *A Dictionary of American Proverbs and Proverbial Phrases, 1820-1880* (Cambridge, Massachusetts: Harvard University Press 1958). Although much of his writing concerned folklore, he also wrote *A History of Bibliographies of Bibliographies* in 1955 and *General Subject-Indexes Since 1548* was published in 1966. Other books and an extraordinary number of articles flowed from his ongoing research, and these were the years before computers and word processing. My sister and I remember alphabetizing yellow 2x3 slips he prepared, one for each proverb or riddle.

Taylor married Alice Jones in 1915, and she bore him three children, Margaret, Richard and Cynthia. Alice sadly died early in 1930, and he married Hasseltine Byrd in 1932 and fathered two more children, Mary Constance and Ann.

A collateral benefit of his teaching position at the University of California was that Taylor could send his professional mail through the University. He carried on a prodigious correspondence with individuals and journals of similar interests around the world. When these individuals came to California, they often stopped to visit and to discuss their scholarship. Former students became close friends, illustrated by the friendship between Wayland Hand and Taylor that lasted the rest of Taylor's life. Many of Taylor's letters are collected at universities and some of the collections are available online.

His large library is now with the University of Georgia in Athens, except his ballad collection which is with the University of California, Berkeley. In addition to collecting books himself, Taylor watched for books and collections that he knew were sought by universities around the world. He might buy and send the desired books or notify the university so it could buy them. He was honored after World War II for his extended efforts to rebuild the university library in Dresden.

Wolfgang Meider published one of the reprints of *The Proverb* and posted a Biographical Sketch that included the following:

> In 1960 Archer Taylor was rightfully and deservedly honored by a most impressive "Festschrift" which his two friends Wayland D.

Hand and Gustave O. Arlt edited with the befitting title *Humaniora, Essays in Literature, Folklore, Bibliography, Honoring Archer Taylor on His Seventieth Birthday* (Locust Valley/New York 1960). The subtitle summarizes Taylor's three major areas of expertise and such internationally renowned contributors as Bartlett Jere Whiting, L. L. Hammerich, Dag Strömbeck, Stith Thompson, Walter Anderson, Taylor Starck, Kurt Ranke, Lutz Röhrich, Matti Kuusi, Georgios A. Megas, Robert Wildhaber, Francis Lee Utley, Anna Brigitta Rooth, Will-Erich Peuckert, Wolfram Eberhard, Julian Krzyzanowski, etc. acknowledge Taylor's worldwide influence.

Influenced by Wayland Hand, the Western States Folklore Society (formerly California Folklore Society) holds annual meetings to encourage professional and amateur folklorists to meet each other, present papers, and engage in discussions of all aspects of folklore and folklife. Since Taylor's 1973 death, the annual meeting has included the Archer Taylor Memorial Lecture. These lectures often reappear as scholarly articles, something that would have pleased Taylor.

Archer Taylor lived and died with friends around the world. He never passed up opportunities to explain and teach—the difference between anecdote and antidote, for example, when a teenage daughter got it wrong. He generously shared his knowledge and curiosity with all.

Ann Taylor Schwing
February 2018

Washington University Studies

NORTHERN PARALLELS TO THE DEATH OF PAN

ARCHER TAYLOR

Associate Professor of German

Plutarch (*De defectu orac.* 17) tells an interesting story of the death of Pan which is reproduced by Sir J. G. Frazer as follows:

In the reign of the emperor Tiberius a certain schoolmaster named Epitherses was sailing from Greece to Italy. The ship in which he had taken passage was a merchantman and there were many other passengers on board. At evening, when they were off the Echinadian Islands, the wind died away, and the vessel drifted in close to the island of Paxos. Most of the passengers were awake, and many were still drinking their wine after dinner, when suddenly a voice hailed the ship from the island, calling upon Thamus. The crew and passengers were taken by surprise, for though there was an Egyptian pilot named Thamus on board, few knew him even by name. Twice the cry was repeated, but Thamus kept silence. At the third call, however, he answered, and the voice from the shore, now louder than ever, said, "When you are come to Palodes, announce that the Great Pan is dead." Astonishment fell upon all, and they consulted whether it would be better to do the bidding of the voice or not. At last Thamus resolved that, if the wind held, he would pass the place in silence, but if it dropped when they were off Palodes, he would give the message. Well, when they were come to Palodes, there was a great calm; so Thamus standing in the stern and looking towards the land cried out, as he had been bidden, "The Great Pan is dead." The words had hardly passed his lips when a loud sound of lamentation broke on their ears, as if a multitude were mourning. This strange story, vouched for by many on board, soon got wind at Rome, and Thamus was sent for and questioned by the emperor Tiberius himself, who caused enquiries to be made about the dead god.

No precise explanation of this story, which, remarks Professor Toy,[1] rests on a misapprehension of some kind, has yet been given. The long list of mythological and theological speculations concerning it have been carefully reviewed not long since by G. A. Gerhard and need not be examined again here.[2] He shows in great detail how from the

[1] *Introduction to the History of Religions*, p. 338.
[2] "Der Tod des grossen Pan," *Sitzungsberichte der Heidelberger Akademie, phil.-hist. Klasse*, V (1915), 5te Abhandlung, pp. 1–52. This monograph is supplemented by his later articles: "Zum Tod des grossen Pan," *Wiener Studien*, XXXVII (1915), 322–52 and "Nochmals zum Tod des grossen Pan," *ibid.*, XXXVIII (1916), 343–76. These articles represent an enormous amount of labor and give an admirably clear survey of the history of the story as a literary motif. With that history I am not concerned, for it is only as regards the ultimate origin of the tale that I differ from Gerhard. Cf. also Fehrle, *Berl. philol. Wochenschrift*, XXXVI (1916), 1468–70. There is a brief, but satisfactory discussion of the story in O. Kurtz, *Beiträge zur Erklärung des volkstümlichen Hexenglaubens in Schlesien*, Diss. (Greifswald), Anklam, 1916, pp. 53 ff. Kurtz terms the story a *Hausgeistsage* in contradiction to the opinion advanced by F. L. W. Schwartz (*Die poetischen Naturanschauungen der Griechen, Römer und Deutschen*, Berlin, 1864–79, II, 140). Schwartz connects the story, at least in one of its special forms, with witches and witchcraft. A long discussion of the story, in which Gerhard's views are adopted and elaborated, may be found in G. Kahlo, *Die Verse in den Sagen und Märchen*, Diss. (Jena), Borna-Leipzig, 1919, pp. 68–77. On the poetical or symbolical employment of the story of Pan's death, with which this article is not concerned, see further R. Basset, "Contes et légendes de la Grèce ancienne," *Rev. des trad. pop.*, XXXII (1917), 219; R. Scot, *Discoveries of Sup-*

time of Eusebius the story has been given a meaning connecting it with Christianity, and how the death of Pan was read as an allegory of the death of Christ, of the collapse of the pagan religions, or of the end of the Devil's power. The fall of paganism as symbolized by Pan's death has proved to be a suggestive simile, particularly for English poets (Spenser, Milton, Mrs. Browning). We may pass over the questions which these interpretations bring with them as well as the problems which concern the special field of Greek religion and mythology: the mortality or the immortality of the Greek gods, the relation of Pan to All-Pan, and the like. A hasty review of what has been said about the story is a necessary introduction to the northern parallels with which this paper is primarily concerned.

At least one analogue (Arabian) to the story of Pan's death has long been known, inasmuch as it was pointed out in 1697 by d'Herbelot; but comparative study may fairly be said to date from Liebrecht's collections in an essay on the Wild Hunt which is appended to his edition (1856) of selections from the *Otia Imperialia* of Gervaise of Tilbury. Liebrecht follows the clue indicated by d'Herbelot. Twenty years later (1875) examination of the tale from the comparative point of view was resumed by Wilhelm Mannhardt in his *Antike Wald- und Feldkulte*, where the first significant assembling of the Germanic parallels as such may be found.

posed *Witchcraft*, London, 1886, p. 513 (an addition in the 1665 ed.); Oscar Wilde's allusion cited in Mutschmann, *Beibl. zur Anglia*, XXX (1919), 304 and in *Palæstra*, C, p. 42; the oration conferring an honorary degree on Robert Browning as quoted on the reverse of the title-page of H. Corson, *Introduction to Browning;* L. Karl, *Mélanges E. Picot*, I, 267–73; J. Plattard, *L'œuvre de Rabelais*, Paris, 1910, pp. 291–94; Wackernagel, *Kleinere Schriften*, II, 107. Reinach's explanation of the story, which I give below, is repeated by Schoff ("Tammuz, Pan, and Christ," *Open Court*, XXVI [1912], 513 ff.) and is copied thence by Van Teslaar ("The Death of Pan," *Psychoanalytic Review*, VIII [1921], 180–83); it is questioned by R. M. Meyer (*Zs. d. Ver. f. Volksk.*, XX [1910], 431). A. F. Chamberlain's article, "The Death of Pan: Poetry and Science," (*Journ. Relig. Psychol.*, V [1912], 87–109) gives nothing that is to the point here.

Since then the appositeness of these analogues has been more or less recognized by mythologists, but there is as yet no thoroughgoing examination of the northern stories for the sake of the light that they may throw on each other and on the Greek version.[3] Gerhard in particular does little more than to bring together the traditions noted by Grimm, Liebrecht, and Mannhardt without adding much from the superabundant store of parallels that have been written down in the course of the last eight centuries.

Plutarch's story contains two elements which lend themselves to comparative study: the message of a mysterious death borne by Thamus and the wailing which the news calls forth on the mainland of Epirus, of which the first is essential to the story, while the second is in comparison incidental. But d'Herbelot and, following him, Liebrecht, Reinach, and others emphasize the second motive because it is paralleled by the wailing for Tammuz and Adonis in Semitic religions. D'Herbelot quotes the following from an Arabian historian, Ben Schonah, whom he terms highly esteemed:

In the year 456 A. H. (1063–64 A.D.) and under the reign of Careim, the twenty-sixth caliph of the Abbasids, there was current in Bagdad a report which spread throughout the whole province of Iraq, that some Turks, while hunting, saw a black tent in the desert. Within the tent there were many persons of both sexes who were beating their cheeks and uttering cries as is customary when some one is dead. Among the cries these words were intelligible: "The great king of the Jinns is dead! Woe upon this land!" A great company of these women then went out to a neighboring cemetery, beating themselves all the while as a sign of sorrow and mourning. And it was believed that any city which failed to bewail the death of the king of the Jinns would be completely destroyed.

Ben Schonah's account is, therefore, an explanation of the origin of a Mesopotamian custom, a custom which

[3] Crusius called for such an "eingehende Betrachtung" thirty years ago in his review of Roscher's *Selene*, cf. *Literarisches Centralblatt*, 1892, col. 62.

has abundant analogues in the Near East, in Syria, Palestine and Egypt. Its similarity to the Greek story extends only to the weeping and the cries, "The great king of the Jinns is dead!" No one is commissioned to bear a message of death to a particular place, and if such an injunction once stood in the account, it has been omitted as inconsistent with the use of the story as an explanation of the ritualistic wailing. Similar stories which make it clear that this custom and its association with an epidemic disease of the throat were rather widely disseminated are reported two centuries later (1203–4 A. D.) from Egypt and Mosul; in these human beings sorrow for the death of the demon, and there is no allusion to a company of supernatural mourners or to the message. A woman of the Jinn (Umm 'Uncud [Mother of the Grape-cluster]), it is explained, had lost her son, and all who failed to bewail his death would fall victims to the plague. Death might be averted by assembling, beating the face, and crying out in a lamenting voice, "O mother of the Grape-cluster, excuse us; the Grape-cluster is dead; we knew it not!" No doubt this rite is, as Robertson Smith observes,[4] a "last survival of an old vintage piaculum." If it is to be connected with the story of Pan, the disappearance of an important feature—the uncomprehended and mysteriously given message of death— are explicable as being due to its etiological employment. It may be observed, of course, that lamentations for a god are a sufficiently well-known characteristic of Semitic worship and ritual, as, for example, the four days of lamentation now referred to Jephthah's daughter (Judges, 11:40) or the wailing for Tammuz (Ezekiel, 8:14). In passing it is

[4] *Religion of the Semites*, pp. 412, 414; Frazer, *Golden Bough*, Pt. III, Dying God, p. 8. Cf. in general A. J. Wensinck, "Some Semitic rites of mourning and religion; studies in their origin and mutual relation," *Kon. Akad. Letterkunde*, N. R., XVIII (1917) and F. Schwally, *Deutsche Literaturzeitung*, 1919, 11–15. Wensinck gives nothing directly referring to this story.

interesting to remark that Miss Jessie Weston brings this ceremonial sorrowing into connection with the legend of the Holy Grail.[5]

The conclusion, then, that some have drawn from the comparison of these Semitic tales and customs with the Greek tale of Pan is that, in one way or another, the Semitic notion of bewailing the death of a god has been adapted to Greek mythology and brought into connection with Pan. The resemblance between Thamus, the name of the pilot, and the Syriac Tammuz is of course a substantial support, for them, of such a transference. But, as was said at the beginning, the comparison seems to be made between the less significant parts of the story, and the Greek tale and the Semitic practises are not so similar, particularly in view of the analogues to be mentioned later, as to render borrowing the sole possible explanation. It is, suggests Sir J. G. Frazer, not beyond the bounds of possibility that the seafarers of Plutarch actually heard the rites of Tammuz being celebrated and that the sounds, wafted across the water, made a startling impression on them.[6]

The numerous and extremely diverse northern parallels, on the other hand, contain almost without exception the more notable motive of the death-message which is incomprehensible to its bearer, while the second motive, the

---

[5] *From Ritual to Romance*, p. 45 and *passim*.

[6] An ingenious explanation offered by W. H. Roscher depends on the goatish nature of Pan. The Egyptian ram-god Mendes, whom the Greeks continually mistook for a goat-god, was worshipped in the form of a living ram, and when it died there was mourning throughout all the land of Thebes. The comparison concerns itself with a wholly incidental part of the story, for in Plutarch's account the goatish nature of Pan is of no significance. Of course in order to maintain this explanation it is necessary to reject all comparisons with stories which others have considered analogous and this Roscher does with complete equanimity, declaring that the coincidence in form between the northern parallels and the death of Pan is accidental and meaningless. Roscher's own explanation, however, has not been widely accepted. See Pauly-Wissowa, *Realenzyklopädie*, s. v. Pan.

weeping for the death of the demon, is less regularly present, although grief seems usually to be implied.[7] A Bavarian example[8] which exhibits a striking resemblance to Plutarch's narrative will illustrate the general type of these stories:

> In Pinzgau a butcher was once walking at midnight down through the hollow road from Saalfelden. Then a voice from the wall of the cliff cried out, "Butcher, when you pass the long cliff at Unken, call into the clefts: 'Salome is dead.'" "I can do that," answered the butcher with a laugh. When he reached the long cliff before day-break, he called his message into it thrice. Then there resounded from the depths of the mountain a loud wailing and sorrowing as of many voices and the butcher hastened on his way full of horror.

The similarity between the two stories is too striking to be rejected as accidental and it cannot, as will be sufficiently clear from what follows, be explained (as Reinach does) as half-learned borrowing from the Greek. The German tale and its congeners either have been handed down from antiquity (as Mannhardt believes) or have sprung from a source common to both the Greek tale and the German. But Maass, who makes the last suggestion casually enough in an essay on Milton's Nativity Ode, does not indicate what this "common source" might be.[9]

Two widely disseminated bits of folk-belief, to one of which he may be referring, have been proposed at different times; Laistner supposed, for this as for so many other tales, the starting-point to be the nightmare (*Alptraum*) and Ger-

---

[7] See the list below; for convenience in what follows I refer to the variants by number. Those which I have been unable to see are marked by an asterisk and are accompanied by an indication of their source.

[8] Variant 46.

[9] Let it be said emphatically and once for all that the equating of the Pan tale with the northern stories is not the subject of the present discussion; that is a matter which can never be demonstrated. The similarity between the Greek story and the folk-tales has been often enough remarked, and it would be a fruitless waste of time and energy to collect more material with the hope of proving the similarity significant.

hard, following Mannhardt and developing his theory, regards as origin the well-nigh universal custom of bewailing the death of the spirits of vegetation. Neither of these explanations is wholly satisfactory: Laistner's deals, it will be seen, with an unessential trait in the story, and many of the creatures in these stories bear no convincing evidence of being descended from vegetation-demons. Gerhard has rejected—and rightly—Laistner's interpretation. Consequently the only explanations in the field are Mannhardt's and, insofar as it is different, Gerhard's modification thereof. These both rest on the fundamental assumption that the story is a vegetation-myth.[10] Possibly Mannhardt would content himself with saying that it is only told of vegetation-demons; and the correctness of that opinion would depend entirely on one's definition of vegetation-demons. Gerhard's argument, however, is based upon the notion that the story is a degenerated and corrupted vegetation-myth, and that conception of it is, I hope to show, erroneous. It is only possible to disprove this assumption by examining the whole body of the traditions, a not inconsiderable bulk of material which has never been brought together, and by showing from it that the story is not inherently a vegetation-myth, but a theme which lends itself to the most varied uses, which developes in the most surprising directions, and which originates in an auditory hallucination. It is obvious that the marked disparity of the forms of the story and their wide circulation presuppose an origin in a very simple idea or phenomenon, which could be conceived or observed in many places, and which lent itself to many uses. The notion of "acousmata," the noises heard in nature which seem to be the voices of men, meets these

[10] The most recent article on the myth of the death of the vegetation demon, a study by a distinguished and competent scholar, omits rather curiously all mention of Gerhard's theories; see Carl Clemen, "Die Tötung des Vegetationsgeistes," *Neue Jahrbücher für das klassische Altertum*, XLIX-L (1922), 120–34.

requirements. The announcement of the mysterious death, which is the starting-point, is an interpretation of the voices in the wind, and, given the first episode, the further course of the story's development is determined by local circumstances. The nature and effect of these local forces and the way in which they combine with the simple idea of the auditory hallucination will be exemplified in detail.

Even if the story can be satisfactorily explained in this way, the explanation does not in the least affect the status of Pan as a demon of vegetation. The demonstration would only prove that the god was powerful enough to attract into his sphere of influence and attach to his name tales which have little to do with his nature—and this phenomenon is frequent enough in mythology and similar popular literature to need no remark and to awaken no surprise. A significant point, however, concerning the Greek story is made by Gerhard in his second article.[11] He observes that Plutarch's narrative conforms with surprizing exactness to Ranke's characterization of German local tradition (*Sage*), which lays claim to credence, as distinguished from the fairy-tale (*Märchen*), which is designed to amuse. The correspondence is point for point. The scene is near the home of the narrator, the time of the action is recent, the credibility of the event is confirmed by mention of the narrator's sources with emphasis on their reliability, particularly on the truthfulness of the one immediately preceding the narrator. Often the teller of the story adds, as does Plutarch, that the actor in the story had had a wee bit too much and so one can believe that he saw more than an ordinary man. These requirements are met by the Greek narrative in an astonishing manner and one is compelled to acknowledge that Plutarch's account, written down centuries ago, agrees exactly with the technique of modern

[11] *Wiener Stud.*, XXXVII (1915), 346.

European local traditions. Both Plutarch's tale and the local traditions to be considered belong to the same genre, and this fact justifies the comparisons which are made below.

The following list of variants mentions practically all instances of the story which have been accessible or which, if not seen, promise for one reason or another to be significant. The geographical extent of the story as revealed by this list calls, perhaps, for some comment. It is not reported, so far as our information goes, from Greece, Italy, Spain, the Netherlands, or France outside the regions where Breton influence is felt in popular tradition. It is impossible to appraise the meaning of these facts. The collectors in some of these countries would, to judge from their labors as published, have disregarded the story as unimportant, if they had heard it. Moreover, all arguments *ex silentio* are risky. The case for the unfamiliarity of the folk with the story seems to be clearest in France, where the collections often include such slight things as it is. A thorough examination of the abundant store of Italian folk-lore might be profitable; at least, the non-appearance of the tale there, if that should be true, would be worthy of remark. In all probability Dutch examples do exist, although none have come under my observation.[12]

LIST OF VARIANTS

Germany.

1. Paul von Winckler, *Der Edelmann*, 1696, pp. 376–77. Cf. Goedeke, *Grundriss der deutschen Dichtung*, III, 260; W. van der Briele, *Paul Winkler* (1630–1686), Diss., Rostock, 1918. See below, p. 30.

2. Frommann, *Die deutschen Mundarten*, II (1855), 565.

---

[12] To be sure, Sepp (*Altbayerischer Sagenschatz*, p. 597) cites a Dutch tale, but his reference seems to be incorrect. See below, pp. 63, 80. Some further quotations (without references) in his *Religion der alten Deutschen*, p. 403 indicate that there are still other (German) versions of the tale which have not been listed below.

*3. R. Bechstein, *Deutsches Sagenbuch*, Leipzig, 1853, p. 236 (cited from Kahlo, *Die Verse in den Sagen und Märchen*, p. 70).

*4. C. and T. Colshorn, *Märchen und Sagen*, Hannover, 1854, pp. 71 ff. (cited from Kahlo, *loc. cit.*).

5. H. B. Forman, *Works of P. B. Shelley*, VI (London, 1880), 212.

North Germany.

6. Kuhn and Schwartz, *Norddeutsche Sagen*, Leipzig, 1848, pp. 162–63, No. 189, 1.

7. *Ibid.*, pp. 163–64, No. 189, 2. The reference in the notes (p. 488) to the *Mirror* has not been identified; the story seems, however, to be the same as No. 128 below.

8. *Ibid.*, p. 289, No. 323.

Pomerania.

9. Jahn, *Volkssagen aus Pommern und Rügen*, Berlin, 1890, p. 80, No. 97.

Silesia and Lusatia.

10. Haupt, "Sagen aus der Ober- und Niederlausitz," *Zs. f. deutsche Mythologie*, IV (1859), 216, No. 6 (reprinted in Haupt, *Sagenbuch der Lausitz*, Leipzig, 1862, I, 36, No. 32 and in R. Kühnau, *Schlesische Sagen*, II (1911), 70–71, No. 736).

11. *Ibid.*, p. 220, No. 13 (reprinted in Haupt, *Sagenbuch der Lausitz*, I, 40, No. 36 and in Kühnau, II, 74-75, No. 741).

12. *Ibid.*, pp. 220-21 (reprinted in Haupt, I, 40, No. 37, Kühnau, II, 179, No. 810. It is taken, says Haupt, verbatim from a chronicle of 1572.

13. Kühnau, *Schlesische Sagen*, II, 182, No. 813.

*14. *Ibid.*, III, No. 1382; cf. O. Kurtz, *Beiträge zur Erklärung des volkstümlichen Hexenglaubens in Schlesien*, Anklam, 1916, pp. 53 ff.

15. *Kohler, *Bilder aus der Oberlausitz*, p. 49 (reprinted in Grässe, *Sagenschatz des Königreichs Sachsen*, II, No. 889 and in Meiche, *Sagenbuch des Königreichs Sachsen*, Leipzig, 1903, p. 349, No. 456).

Prussia.

*16. Temme, *Preussische Sagen*, No. 156.

*17. W. Schwartz, *Sagen und alte Geschichten aus der Mark Brandenburg*[5], Stuttgart, 1909, p. 143 (cited from Kahlo, p. 70).

*18. Engelien and Lahn, *Der Volksmund in der Mark Brandenburg*, Berlin, 1868, p. 22; cf. Kahlo, p. 74.

Mecklenburg.

19. Bartsch, *Sagen, Märchen und Gebräuche aus Mecklenburg*, I (Vienna, 1879), pp. 42–43, No. 61, 3.
20. *Ibid.*, p. 51, No. 71.
21. *Ibid.*, p. 66, No. 84.
21a. *Ibid.*, pp. 80–81, No. 88.
22. *Ibid.*, pp. 87–88, No. 94 (from Niederhöffer, *Mecklenburgs Volkssagen*, Leipzig, 1858–62, IV, 63 f.).
23. *Ibid.*, p. 138, No. 166. Bartsch cites Niederhöffer, IV, 127 as parallel.

Schleswig-Holstein.

24. K. Müllenhoff, *Sagen, Märchen und Lieder der Herzogtümer Schleswig-Holstein und Lauenburg*, Kiel, 1845, p. 291, No. 398.
25. *Ibid.*, p. 291, No. 399 (translated in B. Thorpe, *Northern Mythology*, III, 37–38).
26. *Ibid.*, p. 292, No. 400.
27. *Ibid.*, p. 292, No. 401. Cf. F. Ohrt, *Udvalgte Sønderjydske Folkesagn*, Copenhagen, 1919, pp. 14-15. The story should be classed among the Danish variants, for the region where it was taken down is Danish-speaking and has been given to Denmark by the recent plebiscite.
28. *Ibid.*, pp. 291–292, variant to No. 399 (translated in Thorpe, III, 132-3).
29. *Ibid.*, p. 292, second variant to No. 399.
*30. Sophie Klörss, *Lieder und Balladen*, 1909, p. 62, "Elfkönigsbraut." A literary version, cited by Gerhard, *Wiener Studien*, XXXVII (1915), 348, n. 2.
31. L. Strackerjan, *Aberglaube und Sagen aus dem Herzogtum Oldenburg*, zweite erweiterte Ausgabe von K. Willoh, Oldenburg, 1909, I, 405, §220 d.
32. *Ibid.*, I, 406, §220 k.
33. *Ibid.*, I, 492–3, §257 f.
34. *Ibid.*, p. 493, §257 f.
35. *Ibid.*, I, 493–4, §257 f.

Westphalia.

36. A. Kuhn, *Sagen, Gebräuche und Märchen aus Westfalen*, Leipzig, 1859, I, 246–48, No. 282.

The Harz.

37. H. Pröhle, *Harzsagen*[2], Leipzig, 1886, pp. 7–8, No. 10.
38. *Ibid.*, p. 50, No. 80.
39. *Ibid.*, p. 145, No. 157.

The Rhine.

40. O. Schell, *Bergische Sagen*, Elberfeld, 1897, pp. 235–36, No. 219 (from Montanus-Waldbrühl, *Vorzeit*, I, 83). It may also be found in Waldbrühl, *Wesen der niederrheinischen Sagen*, pp. 14–15; see Schell, p. 585.

Hesse.

*41. Lyncker, *Deutsche Sagen und Sitten in hessischen Gauen*, Kassel, 1854, p. 55, No. 88.

*Thuringia.**

42. Bange, *Thüringische Chronik*, fol. 49ᵃ (reprinted in Grimm, *Deutsche Sagen*, II, 185, No. 485). On this see Mannhardt, *Antike Wald- und Feldkulte*, I, 93; Liebrecht, *Zur Volkskunde*, p. 257; and Gerhard, p. 37.

Saxony.

43. J. and W. Grimm, *Deutsche Sagen*,[4] 1905, p. 49, No. 69*. From *Anekdoten der Charlotte Elisabeth von Orleans*, Strassburg, 1789, pp. 133–34, cf. *Elisabeth Charlotte von Orleans*, Leipzig, 1820, p. 386. Although not published until the end of the century, the tale was written down in a letter of 1719. Gerhard (*Wiener Studien*, XXXVII [1915], 350) suggests Ponickau as the place meant by Bonikau.

44. A. Witzschel, *Sagen aus Thüringen* (*Kleine Beiträge zur deutschen Mythologie, Sitten- und Heimatskunde*, I), 1866, p. 106, No. 100.

45. J. G. T. Grässe, *Sagenschatz des Königreichs Sachsen*, Dresden, 1855, p. 552, No. 707 (the same in Grohmann, *Sagen aus Böhmen*, Prag, 1863, pp. 177 ff. from Vernaleken, *Mythen und Bräuche des Volkes in Oesterreich*, Vienna, 1859, pp. 218–20, No. 39). The common source is presumably Peschek (*Büschings Wöchentliche Nachrichten*, I, 72 ff., 97 ff., 291, 294). The story is reprinted in Henne-am-Rhyn, *Die deutsche Volkssage*[2], pp. 320–22; Preusker, *Blicke in die vaterländische Vorzeit*, Leipzig, 1841, I, 57; Meiche, *Sagenbuch des Königreichs Sachsen*, 1903, p. 332, No. 434; Haupt, *Sagenbuch der Lausitz*, I, 32, No. 27; Kühnau, *Schlesische Sagen*, II, 171, No. 83.

* My number 44 should have been placed under this rubric.

Bavaria.

46. F. Panzer, *Beitrag zur deutschen Mythologie: Bayerische Sagen und Gebräuche,* Munich, 1855, II, 45, No. 54 (reprinted in Freissauff, *Salzburger Volkssagen,* Vienna, 1880, p. 13).

47. *Ibid.,* pp. 48–49, No. 63 (reprinted *ibid.,* p. 189).

48. *Ibid.,* p. 197, No. 340.

49. *Ibid.,* p. 197, No. 341.

50. Schöppner, *Sagenbuch der bayerischen Lande,* Munich, 1852, II, 26 (reprinted in Wolf, *Beiträge,* II, 280).

51. J. N. Sepp, *Altbayerischer Sagenschatz,* Munich, 1876, p. 595 (reprinted in Freissauff, *Salzburger Sagen,* 1880, p. 212). I have not seen H. Müller, *Moenus,* pp. 35 ff. to which Sepp refers.

52. *Ibid.,* p. 598–99. Cf. *Wiener Studien,* XXXVII, 350.

53. K. Reiser, *Sagen, Gebräuche und Sprichwörter des Allgäus,* Kempten, I (1903), p. 130, §131.[13]

54. *Ibid.,* p. 132, §132.

55. *Ibid.,* pp. 133–34, §133.

56. *Ibid.,* p. 136, §135.

57. *Ibid.,* p. 136, §135, 2.

58. *Ibid.,* p. 136, §136.

59. *Ibid.,* pp. 141–2, §142.

60. *Ibid.,* p. 142–3, §143.

61. *Ibid.,* p. 143, §144.

Franconia (Voigtland).

62. R. Eisel, *Sagenbuch des Voigtlands,* Gera, 1871, p. 145 (reprinted in Henne-am-Rhyn², p. 158, No. 235 a).

The Palatinate.

63. F. X. Schönwerth, *Aus der Oberpfalz,* Augsburg, 1858, II, 366, §10.

*64. *Ibid.,* reprinted by Henne-am-Rhyn², p. 287, No. 437 without giving reference to page.

Swabia.

65. E. Meier, *Deutsche Sitten, Sagen und Gebräuche aus Schwaben,* Stuttgart, 1852, p. 20, No. 11 (reprinted in Henne-am-Rhyn², p. 286, No. 435).

---

[13] According to Kahlo (p. 72) some of Reiser's tales are reprinted in H. Eggert, *Allgäuer Sagen,* Kempten, 1914, pp. 19 ff., 247.

Baden.

66. Baader, *Volkssagen aus Baden*, p. 20, No. 26 (reprinted in F. Ranke, *Die deutschen Volkssagen*, IV, 281).

Switzerland.

67. D. Jäcklin, *Volkstümliches aus Graubünden*, Chur, 1916, pp. 107–8 (cf. ed. Zürich, 1874, I, 19).

*68. M. Tscheinen and P. J. Ruppin, *Walliser Sagen*, Sitten, 1871, p. 204, No. 95 (reprinted in Ranke, *Die deutschen Volkssagen*, IV, 281; not in Tscheinen and Ruppin, *Walliser Sagen*, Brig, 1907). Cf. *Wiener Studien*, XXXVII (1915), 351, n. 4.

69. E. L. Rochholz, *Schweizersagen aus dem Aargau*, I, 275, No. 6, cf. p. 346.

70. *Ibid.*, I, 317-18, No. 226. The same story may be found in Henne-am-Rhyn, *Die deutsche Volkssage*[2], p. 345, No. 532 and in Herzog, *Schweizersagen*, Aarau, 1913, II, 140–41, No. 127. Rochholz cites further: *Alpenrosen*, 1827, p. 310; *Wanderer in der Schweiz*, 1840, p. 381: *Helvetia*, Volkskalendar von Reithard, 1852, p. 188: Kohlrusch, *Schweizerisches Sagenbuch*, I, No. 37.

71. A. Lütolf, *Sagen aus den fünf Orten*, Luzern, 1862, p. 496, No. 455.

72. *Kuenlin, *Alpenblumen und Volkssagen aus dem Greierzerland*, Sursee, 1834, p. 25 (cited by Haupt, *Zs. f. d. Mythol.*, IV [1859], 216). Kohlrusch (*Schweizerisches Sagenbuch*, 1854, pp. 149–50, No. 11) reprints the story and cites page 95. It may also be found in Herzog, *Schweizersagen*, I, 82, No. 81 (3rd ed., I, 109, No. 85).

73. Herzog, *Schweizersagen*[3], Aarau, 1913, I, 59-60, No. 45.

73a. Herzog, *Schweizersagen*, 1871, p. 42, No. 43.

Vorarlberg.

74. Vonbun, *Volkssagen aus Vorarlberg*[2], Innsbruck, 1850, pp. 2–3, No. 3 (reprinted in Vonbun, *Die Sagen Vorarlbergs*, 1858, pp. 13–14, No. 15).

75. *Ibid.*, p. 7, No. 5 (reprinted *ibid.*, p. 4, No. 2). Cf. Junghans, *Alpenmärchen*, Stuttgart-Cannstadt, n.d., p. 6.

76. Vonbun, *Sagen Vorarlbergs*, 1858, p. 4, No. 1.

77. Vonbun, *Beiträge zur deutschen Mythologie*, Chur, 1862, p. 48.

*78. Vonbun, *Sagen Vorarlbergs*, 1889, p. 52. Cited in Zingerle, *Sagen aus Tirol*[2], 1891, p. 599, No. 50.

Tyrol.

79. *Zimmersche Chronik* (ed. Barack), IV, 283. Cf. Liebrecht, *Germania*, XIV (1868), 404.

80. I. V. and J. Zingerle, "Sagen aus Tirol," *Zs. f. d. Mythol.*, I (1853), 461, No. 1 (reprinted in Zingerle, *Sagen aus Tirol²*, 1891, p. 55, No. 81).

81. *Ibid.*, pp. 461–62, No. 2 (reprinted *ibid.*, p. 53, No. 77).

82. *Ibid.*, p. 462, No. 3 (reprinted *ibid.*, p. 55, No. 82).

83. *Ibid.*, p. 462, No. 4 (reprinted *ibid.*, p. 54, No. 79). Cf. Mannhardt, I, 92.

84. I. V. Zingerle, "Sagen aus Tirol," *Zs. f. d. Mythol.*, II (1855), 60, No. 16 (reprinted *ibid.*, pp. 34–35, No. 50).

85. Alpenburg, *Deutsche Alpensagen*, Vienna, 1861, pp. 164–65, No. 167.

86. *Ibid.*, p. 209, No. 212.

87. Alpenburg, *Mythen und Sagen Tirols*, Zürich, 1857, p. 67, No. 5.

88. *Ibid.*, p. 68, No. 6 (reprinted in F. Ranke, *Die deutschen Volkssagen*, IV, 177, [cf. p. 281] and in P. Zaunert, *Deutsche Natursagen*, I, 68–69 [cf. p. 141]).

89. *Ibid.*, p. 68, No. 7.

*90. Zingerle, *Sagen, Märchen und Gebräuche aus Tirol*, p. 25, No. 30.

*91. *Ibid.*, p. 32, No. 42.

92. L. von Hörmann, *Mythologische Beiträge aus Wälschtirol*, Innsbruck, 1870, p. 9.

93. C. Hauser, *Sagen aus dem Paznaun und dessen Nachbarschaft*, Innsbruck, 1894, pp. 11–12, No. 8.

*94. Schneller, *Märchen und Sagen aus Wälschtirol*, Innsbruck, 1867, p. 210, No. 4.

*95. *Ibid.*, p. 212, No. 7.

*96. *Ibid.*, p. 217. Cf. Liebrecht, *Heidelberger Jahrbücher*, LXI (1868), 311.

97. I. V. Zingerle, *Sagen aus Tirol²*, Innsbruck, 1891, p. 46, No. 69.

98. *Ibid.*, p. 46, No. 70.

99. *Ibid.*, p. 47, No. 71.

100. *Ibid.*, p. 48, No. 72.

101. *Ibid.*, p. 49, No. 73.

102. *Ibid.*, pp. 103–4, No. 168.
103. *Ibid.*, p. 123, No. 198.
104. *Ibid.*, pp. 601–2, variant to No. 71.
105. *Ibid.*, p. 602, variant to No. 72.
106. *Ibid.*, p. 618, variant to No. 198.
107. P. Zaunert, *Deutsche Natursagen*, I (Jena, 1921), 141 (from Dörler, *Zs. f. österreichische Volksk.*, III, 290).

Carinthia.

108. Rappold, *Sagen aus Kärnten*, Augsburg, 1887, p. 41. This reference seems to be incorrect.
109. Graber, *Sagen aus Kärnten*, Leipzig, 1914, p. 48, No. 54.
110. *Ibid.*, p. 161, No. 204.

Styria.

111. J. Krainz, *Mythen und Sagen aus dem steirischen Hochlande*, Bruck a. d. Mur, 1880, p. 393, No. 299.

Salzburg.

112. Freissauff, *Salzburger Volkssagen*, Vienna, 1880, pp. 139–40.
113. *Ibid.*, p. 193.
114. *Ibid.*, p. 194.
115. *Ibid.*, p. 195–96.
116. *Ibid.*, p. 212. Cf. No. 51 above.

Bohemia.

117. Grohmann, *Sagen aus Böhmen*, Prag, 1863, p. 227 (from Krolmus, *Starocesk. Povest.*, II, 42).
118. Vernaleken, *Mythen und Bräuche*, 1859, p. 26, No. 8; cf. Mannhardt, II, 174.
Cf. No. 40 above.

England.

119. William Baldwin, *Beware the Cat*, ca. 1560; ed. J. O. Halliwell, 1864 (in ten copies only); ed. Thos. Corser, *Collectanea Anglo-Poetica*, Part I (1860), pp. 112 ff. (Chetham Soc.). Cf. W. E. A. Axon, *Cheshire Gleanings*, London, 1884, pp. 139 ff.; Brie, *Anglia*, XXXVII (1913), 317 ff.; "Old Irish Words and Deeds," *Dublin Univ. Mag.*, LXXIV (1869), 324–26.
120. *Ibid.*, cf. Brie, *Anglia*, XXXVII, 317; Wood-Martin, *Traces of the Elder Faiths of Ireland*, II (1902), 124–25.

*121. Grose as cited by Fitzgerald, *Revue des trads. pop.*, IV (1889), 83.

*122. Lord Littleton's Letters as cited by Sir Walter Scott, Notes to the *Lady of the Lake*, Note I (Houghton, Mifflin ed., II, 323).

*123. Sir Walter Scott told the story to Irving. Cf. Agnes Repplier, *The Fireside Sphinx*, p. 34; I do not find the reference to this conversation.

124. Southey, *The Doctor*, VII, "Memoirs of a Cat's Eden."

125. P. P., *Notes and Queries*, 1st Ser., vi, 70 (reprinted in *Choice Notes*, p. 26).

126. *Ibid.*, 1st Ser., xi, 398 (reprinted in Timbs, *Abbeys*, I, 485; *Choice Notes*, p. 73; Mrs. H. P. Whitcombe, *Bygone Days in Devon and Cornwall*. p. 154; Courtney, *Cornish Feasts and Folk-Lore*, p. 125).

127. Pusseyite, *ibid.*, 2nd Ser., xi, 36 (12 Jan., 1861; Lancs.).

128. D. C., *ibid.*, 2nd Ser., x, 463 (15 Dec., 1860) and reprinted in Dyer, *Eng. Folklore*, p. 110; Harland and Wilkinson, *Lancashire Legends, Traditions, and Pageants*, London, 1873, pp. 12–3 (South Lancs.). See above No. 7.

129. Burne, "Two Folk-Tales Told by a Herefordshire Squire in 1845–6," *Folk-Lore Journal*, II (1884), 22–23 (reprinted in Hartland, *English Folk- and Fairy-Tales*, pp. 126–7 and in E. M. Leather, *Folk-Lore of Herefordshire*, Hereford, 1912, p. 176).

130. [C. J. T.,] *Folklore and Legends: English* (pub. Gibbings, London, 1890), pp. 150–55. This is the chief basis of J. Jacobs, *More English Fairy Tales*, pp. 157 ff.; cf. notes, p. 237.

131. J. O. Halliwell, *Popular Rhymes and Nursery Tales*, London 1849, p. 51.

132. Halfdon, *Academy*, XXIV, No. 587 (Aug. 4, 1883), p. 81; cf. pp. 99, 115, 231.

133. *Saturday Magazine*, X (1837), 44–46: Dr. Leyden's version; cf. No. 149 below.

Ireland.

134. Fitzgerald, *Rev. des trad. pop.*, IV (1889), 82. He remarks that he has collected about a score of modern Anglo-Irish versions.

135. *Ibid.*, pp. 83–84.

136. *Ibid.*, pp. 84–85.

137. L. Brueyre, *Contes de la Grande Bretagne*, Paris, 1875, p. 354, No. 90 (from Kennedy).

138. Lady Wilde, *Ancient Legends, Mystic Charms and Superstitions of Ireland*, London, 1902, p. 153.

139. Lady Gregory, *Visions and Beliefs of the West of Ireland*, New York, 1920, II, 272 (Co. Galway).
140. Pusseyite, *Notes and Queries*, 2nd Ser., xi, 36 (12 Jan., 1861; Co. Meath).
141. Wood-Martin, *Traces of the Elder Faiths*, II, 9–10.
142. *Ibid.*, pp. 10–11 (from C. J. Hamilton, *Spectator*, Apr. 9, 1897).
143. Larminie, *West Irish Folk-Tales*, London, 1893, pp. 70–73.
144. *Ibid.*, pp. 100–103.
145. *Ibid.*, p. 153.

Scotland.

146. J. G. Campbell, *Witchcraft and Second Sight in the Highlands and Islands of Scotland*, Glasgow, 1902, p. 38.
147. *Ibid.*, pp. 38–39.
148. *Ibid.*, p. 39.
149. Dr. Leyden's version may be found in *Quarterly Review*, XXI (1819), 98 and translated in *Rev. des trad. pop.*, V (1890), 198. See above No. 133.

Denmark.

150. Thiele, *Danmarks Folkesagn*, Copenhagen, 1843, II, 187–88. Cf. Repplier, *Fireside Sphinx*, p. 34; Keightley, Fairy Mythology, pp. 120–21; *Saturday Magazine*, X (1837), 44.
151. *Ibid.*, pp. 205–6. Cf. B. Thorpe, *Northern Mythology*, III, 132.
152. *Ibid.*, p. 207 (reprinted in Rask, *Morskabslæsning for den Danske Almue*, 1840, p. 735).
*153. Larsen, *Odds og Skippinge Herreder*, p. 97. Cited by Thiele.
154. Mannhardt, *Antike Wald- und Feldkulte*, II, 172.
155. Grundtvig, *Gamle danske Minder*, III (1861), 90.
156. E. T. Kristensen, *Danske Sagn som de har lydt i Folkemunde*, I(Aarhus, 1892), p. 76, No. 300.
157–168. *Ibid.*, pp. 76–80, Nos. 302–13.[14]
169. *Ibid.*, pp. 80–81, No. 314.
170. *Ibid.*, p. 81, No. 315.
171. *Ibid.*, p. 81, No. 316.
172. *Ibid.*, p. 81, No. 317.
173–174. *Ibid.*, pp. 81–82, No. 318–19.
175–177. *Ibid.*, pp. 82–83, Nos. 320–322.

[14] Kristensen's collection contains some 65 versions of the story. I cite the versions in groups except where I have discussed a particular tale.

178-181. *Ibid.*, pp. 83-84, Nos. 323-26.
182. *Ibid.*, p. 84, No. 327.
183-197. *Ibid.*, pp. 84-88, Nos. 328-42.
198. *Ibid.*, p. 88, No. 343.
199-202. *Ibid.*, pp. 88-89, Nos. 344-47.
203. *Ibid.*, p. 89, No. 348.
204-207. *Ibid.*, pp. 89-91, Nos. 349-52.
208. *Ibid.*, p. 91, No. 353.
209. *Ibid.*, p. 91, No. 354.
210-219. *Ibid.*, pp. 91-95, Nos. 355-64.
220. *Ibid.*, p. 95, No. 368.
221. *Ibid.*, p. 95, No. 369.
222. *Ibid.*, p. 321, No. 1066.

Norway.

223. Asbjörnsen, *Norske Huldre-eventyr og Folkesagn*,[3] Christiana, 1870, p. 45. Cf. Liebrecht, *Heidelberger Jahrbücher*, LXV (1872), 845.
224. *Ibid.*, p. 47.
225. *Ibid.*, pp. 307-8.
226. *Runa* (ed. Dybeck), July, 1844, p. 44.
227. *Olafssaga Tryggvasonar*, ch. liii. There is another version derived from the *Olafssaga* in *Fornmannasögur*, Copenhagen, 1825, I, 211 ff., ch. cii ff. Cf. Longfellow, *Tales of a Wayside Inn* and Varnhagen, *Longfellows Tales of a Wayside Inn und ihre Quellen*, Berlin, 1884, pp. 60 ff., "The Musician's Tale: The Saga of King Olaf."

France.

228. Sébillot, *Traditions et superstitions de la Haute Bretagne*, Paris, 1882 (Les littératures populaires, IX), I, 139-40.
229. *Ibid.*, II, 47-8. Cf. Liebrecht, *Zs. f. rom. philol.*, VI (1882), 453-4.
230. *Ibid.*, II, 48, n. 1.
231. *Ibid.*, II, 48-9.
*232. G. Dottin, *Les Parlers du Bas-Maine*, p. 432.
233. Le Men, "Traditions et superstitions de la Basse Bretagne," *Revue celtique*, I (1870-72), 240.
*234. Taylor and Nodier, *Voyage pittoresque*. (Cited by Gerhard, p. 36, n. 4.)
*235. G. Sand, *Légendes rustiques*, p. 155. (Cited by Sébillot, Traditions, II, 49.)

236. Duynes, "Légendes et superstitions du Pays du Dol," *Revue des traditions populaires*, VIII (1893), 372.

237. "Coûtumes et superstitions de la Haute-Bretagne, No. 47, Folklore du clos poulet," *Revue des traditions populaires*, XVIII (1903), 446.

238. Harou, "Notes sur les superstitions de la province de Liège," *ibid.*, XVIII (1903), 477.

239. Pluquet, *Contes populaires de l'arrondissement de Bayeux*,² p. 14 (reprinted in A. Bosquet, *La Normandie romanesque*, Paris, 1845, pp. 138–9).

*240. "Briefe aus der Normandie, Bayeux," *Ausland*, 7 Sept., 1857.

241. Sébillot, *Contes*, I, 310.

242. Sébillot, "Contes résumés de la Haute Bretagne," *Revue des traditions populaires*, IX (1894), 349, No. 64.

Canada (French).

243. Barbeau, "Anecdotes de Gaspé, de la Beauce, et de Témiscouata," *Journal of American Folklore*, XXXIII (1920), 190–1, No. 161.

Guernsey (French).

244. Teeling, "Guernsey Folklore," *Gentleman's Magazine*, CCXCIII (1902), 17 ff.

245. MacCulloch, *Guernsey Folklore* (ed. E. F. Carey), London, 1903, pp. 213–4.

246. *Ibid.*, p. 214.

It is obviously out of the question to examine all or any large part of these two hundred and forty tales. Nor would the discussion be profitable. In the following pages I shall endeavor to illustrate the more clearly marked groups into which they subdivide themselves and to point out the special characteristics of each group. By this method it will be possible to show that the story has undergone many local modifications and that it enters, in one region or another, into a surprising variety of combinations with other, unrelated themes. When these facts are recognized, it will follow as a matter of course that no one of the local modifications or combinations can be chosen, without convincing reasons for the selection, as representative of the primitive form of the story. Yet, owing to the previous insufficient collections, this error is just the one which has been committed. As a result, the tales have been interpreted to fit theories, although such theories do not afford a satisfactory explanation of the texts taken as a whole. I begin with the tales which have the simplest form and pass to the more involved combinations. Two distinct types of the story and one tale, which has some obscure connection with it, are treated in this fashion. The first type is represented by those stories in which the actors possess human form, and the second by those in which the actors are cats. Finally, a tale which deals with news of a fire is considered briefly.

Perhaps the simplest form in which the tale can appear is that which it assumes when it is told in almost purely human terms (granting of course the initial auditory illusion, which is not within everyday experience). The night wanderer hears the cries, and since he does not understand their significance he repeats them at home as a curiosity. Some one of his auditors proves to be greatly affected by the news, although the reason for his (or her) emotion is not always made plain. Such is a dwarf story from Lusatia:

> A dwarf once came to the owner of a farm situated on the Dettersberg and while he was plowing asked him to tell Hübel [fem.] that Habel [masc.] was dead. While the man is telling this strange adventure at his midday meal a little woman whom he had never seen before appeared in one corner of the room and hastened out of the house and up the mountain with loud lamentation. She was never seen again.[15]

It does not appear that this creature, who was no doubt supernatural, had any particular function in the household, nor is any reason given for the selection of such a queer way in which to communicate the news to her. Possibly,

[15] Variant 10.

although it is not obvious, she was a friendly cobold; but in that event her disappearance might be expected to affect the household's prosperity.

In Denmark also such creatures, of whose existence the residents in the house have been ignorant, make their presence known in a similar fashion, as for example in the following story:

> A man from Sönderholm had been in Aalborg and was coming home. When he passed Trold kirke a dwarf came out, clapped its hands, and said, "Greet Ati and say that Wati is dead!" He told this at home and added, "I do not know who this might be." Then some one came out of a chest standing on the floor and said while he walked up and down on the floor clapping his hands, "Ah, is Wati dead, is Wati dead."[16]

The immediately succeeding variant in Kristensen's collection[17] differs only in negligible matters from the preceding one, but it is very significant because it shows how the story may have originated. When the message, which is communicated by the voice of some one unseen, is announced in the house, it is answered by wailing behind the stove, while at the same time, "*it* went out the door like a puff of wind." Here no supernatural person at all occurs and the whole is capable of a purely physical explanation.

Quite as curious is an instance of a forest-woman (*Holzweiblein*) who took refuge for the winter in a man's house near Königshain in Upper Lusatia. In the spring another woman of the same kind came to the window and cried, "Deuto!" whereupon the first comer departed in tears.[18] This rather confused and stupid incident is apparently the

---

[16] Variant 180. These names, Ati and Wati, appear to be characteristic of a large group of the Danish variants, and they are also known in Schleswig among German speaking people. Cf. Kristensen, *Danske Sagn*, pp. 83 ff., Nos. 323–350 (not all contain this particular pair of names). Here also belong the Atfod and Vatfod of Variant 154. Cf. Variant 26. Another name frequent in these northern stories (Danish) is Bilser (Pilser, Balser, Baldter, etc.).

[17] Variant 181.

[18] Variant 12.

oldest German version, for it dates from 1572. Another story[19] of the usual type, of a much later date, is also localized in the same village. According to it the two last surviving *Buschmännchen*, who lived in the last house in the village, were seen at infrequent intervals. Finally one appeared, sobbing, "Hipelpipel is dead!" and was thenceforth seen no more.—The first of these Lusatian tales may perhaps be looked upon as confirming the explanation I have offered: the meaningless cry, "Deuto!"—another version[20] has "Deutosen!"—might be interpreted as an auditory illusion out of which the story-teller has not tried to make sense.[21] Vonbun has taken down an instance[22] in which the message seems pretty clearly to have originated in such an illusion:

Jochrumpla of Samangerberg, a *Fenggi* (forest-woman), came to Hanskasper and offered herself as a maid, saying that she could not stay at home on account of quarreling with her husband. She proved to be very satisfactory. "After three years there came one night a knocking and calling at Hanskasper's window: 'Jochrumpla, come home, Muggastutz is dead.'" She ran off in the direction of the Samangerberg.

The names appearing in this story attach it to a large group of tales to be considered later.[23] There is at least one version in which we do not learn the message. This is a variation which is easily explained, for the narrator is unable or unwilling to recall the meaningless words of the demon and simply omitted them. The story does not suffer from the change.

[19] Variant 11.
[20] Variant 15.
[21] Compare another confused Silesian tale (Variant 13): A *Holzweibel* spent the winter regularly with a certain family. When the plant called Lichel sprouted in the spring, a forest-man appeared and called, "Lichel, come out!" She rose sadly and said, "When Lichel comes out, I must go," and went off with the man. The episode seems to have been repeated annually (an obscured vegetation-myth?).
[22] Variant 76.
[23] See below pp. 46 ff.

A little servant maid (*Erdweibchen*) employed by a family resident in the valley of the Aar was working in the fields one day. While she was carrying home on her head a heavy bundle of hay a little man of the same species came to meet her and whispered a word in her ear. Without speaking she laid aside her load and went off with him, never to be seen again.[24]

Common to this last story and to all mentioned thus far is the absence of any supernatural flavor in the narrative; it is thoroughly anthropomorphized. A striking instance of this tendency to dispense with superhuman elements is to be seen in a French (Breton) tale, in which the death-message is adapted to fit the local type of malicious elf, called *lutin*. These creatures enjoy stealing apples, spilling wheat, and damaging crops. The narrative sounds like an experience of a hasty-tempered farmer with a crowd of mischievous urchins:

A farmer resented the losses the *lutins* were causing him and took advantage of the opportunity when he saw one of them bending over to dig his potatoes. He snatched up a large stick and stealing up behind the elf, hit it over the head so that it fell face down. At once its companions, who have watched the scene, cried "Coiffette est morte! Coiffette est morte!" and pursued the murderer with such zeal that he barely escaped from their clutches.[25]

The sorrow of the vanishing demon is made more intelligible by explaining that the mysterious death has occurred in its family. Thus, in a story[26] from Tyrol, the auditor of the message does not seem to be at the slightest loss in identifying the person for whom the message is intended:

There was a maid who was descended from the stock of the forest-demons (*Norggen*) and who gave wise advice in matters concerning wind and weather, baking, sowing, and the like. Once when the peasant with whom she lived was riding home late at night through the forest he heard a voice saying, "Hoss, Hoss, on your snow-white horse, tell

[24] Rochholz, *Schweizersagen aus dem Aargau*, I, 275–6, No. 187.
[25] Variant 228.
[26] Variant 82. The story surely belongs with the changeling group cited below, pp. 39–40.

Hanne her father is dead." When he came home he told the maid the news and she began to lament and wail and disappeared forever.

The way in which the peasant is addressed links this story with others told in the same region about changelings. The message, "Kielkopf, sage doch Torke, er solle nach Hause kommen, sein Kind sei todt!" which occurs in a North German story,[27] caused Torke, an invisible, bread-stealing dwarf to depart in such haste that he dropped a a bag of dough. A Thuringian tale[28] is clearly descended from the same original story for the message, although a little altered, agrees in the use of a similar name: "Sag' Kielkehl seine Frau sei krank und werde bald sterben." On hearing the news a gnome crept from under the bed. For the effectiveness of the story it is necessary that the creature addressed should have some clear relation both to the individual with whom it is staying and to the person who is alleged to be dead, although, as we have seen, there are instances which comply with neither of these requirements.

On account of the whimsical names it is especially likely to be brought into the cycle of Tom-tit-tot or Rumpelstiltzchen, that class of tales in which a demon keeps its name secret and a sudden change in its fortunes is accomplished by the disclosure of the hidden name. An example of this is a tale from Tyrol collected by Zingerle:

A maid who kept her name secret and who was teased by a *Nörklein* (demon) in various ways dwelt with a peasant in Andrian. Once the peasant went out into the forest to cut wood. While there he suddenly heard a voice crying, "Woodsman, woodsman, tell Giragingele that Hörele is dead." He noted these words and at supper, when he had returned home, told the story and said jestingly to the maid, "Now we know your name." She had hardly heard the words of the peasant when she ran out and disappeared forever.[29]

[27] Variant 6.
[28] Variant 44.
[29] Variant 81.

The emphasis of the story is altered: the news of the death awakens no emotion in the maid and apparently only the discovery of her name causes her embarrassment. She is of course conceived as a friendly, house-haunting demon, who wishes her name kept secret.[30] A similar creature is mentioned in the following story from Baden[31] which, as we shall see later, is a not entirely satisfactory representative of a rather large class of these tales. (For the present note merely the name "Yoke-bearer" as a characteristic token of this group.)

An invisible voice called to a farmer who was going home from the field with a yoke on his shoulder, "Yoke-bearer! Tell Gloria the *Kanzelmann* is dead!" At supper he told his experience to the maid, adding, "Now we know that your name is Gloria." Straightway she jumped up from the table and was never seen again.

It is clear enough from what has been said that it is impossible to start from such a tale as this to explain the story. Laistner makes such an effort, but in so doing he is obliged to restrict himself to a single type, the present one, of our story.[32] How the combination ever came to be made

---

[30] Sepp (*Altbayerischer Sagenschatz*, p. 599, n. 1) observes that *giragingelen* means to play blind's man buff—but the significance of this fact escapes me.

[31] Variant 66.

[32] In Tyrol and the Hinterstein valley of Allgäu a seemingly very remote parallel of this story is told. It is accepted by Gerhard and Laistner as an analogue. Although it has been taken down at least three different times, it seems a very flat and worthless thing. The story is:

A "wild woman" is married to a peasant from whom she conceals her name. One day while she is combing her children, another "wild woman," who is passing by, stops and says in a sad voice:
"O my dear Gertraud,
How the worms are eating your plants."
Those who are about hear her name and so she must leave. See F. Ranke, *Die deutschen Volkssagen*, p. 81 (from Zingerle, *Sagen, Märchen, und Gebräuche*, 1859, p. 34, No. 43); I. Zingerle, "Sagen aus Tirol," *Zs. f. d. Myth.*, II (1855), 183, No. 28 (reprinted in I. V. Zingerle, *Sagen aus Tirol*², Innsbruck, 1891, pp. 49–50, No. 75). Cf. K. Reiser, *Sagen, Gebräuche und Sprichwörter des Allgäus*, I, 130–31, §132; Laistner, *Rätsel der Sphinx*, I, 208.

appears from a Tyrolese tale[33] in which the adding of the new motif, the disclosure of the hidden name, is almost prepared for. The story is as follows:

A girl came to the innkeeper on the Moosstrasse late one evening and begged for shelter and employment as a maid. His wife thought her hands too tender, but finally yielded to her pleas. Prosperity now began for the household. The girl came to be regarded by all as the daughter of the house, although no one could learn anything about her origin or family. One day a wood-cutter came to the inn and asked for the girl. When she came he reported that he had heard a cry from a cleft in the rocks, "Peasant, tell the maid at the Moos Inn, her cousin is dead!" She departed without a word of farewell, but prosperity remained with the innkeeper.

The creature may be thought of, moreover, as a friendly elf, appearing in the household as a maid; of this examples have been given, and perhaps one more[34] will suffice:

One day a farmer went to Lienz, and he heard a voice call down from the cliff, "Hello, peasant, tell Vef' (fem.) Trud is dead." He did not understand the meaning of the words and when he had returned he narrated his experience at the midday meal. Then the maid arose and said: "I must now go. You, mistress, take my spoon to skim the milk and be blessed in it." Then she vanished. But the spoon is said to have actually brought prosperity into the household.

The oldest printed version of our story, that in Paul von Winckler's *Der Edelmann* (1696), belongs to this type. It is as follows:

[Es spricht der Herr Licentiat:] "Worbey ich denn meinen Herren etwas gleichlautendes mittheilen wil/ so mir nunmehr vor 24. Jahren/ in dem damaligen Dähnisch-Schwedischen Kriege/ ein so vornehmer als gewissenhaffter/ allem Aberglauben abge-[p. 377] fryter Mann erzehlet/ dass ich an dessen Warheit keinen Zweiffel zu setzen habe. Dieser war mein Obrister/ und versicherte mich auf sein Christliches Gewissen/ dass als er damals vor etlich und dreissig Jahren/ unter dem Ehrwürdigsten dähnischen Könige Christian dem Vierdten/ Lieutenant gewesen/ und einsmals des Mittags gegen 12. Uhr/ in Holstein bey einem

[33] Variant 112.
[34] Variant 110.

bekandten/ unweit Schlesswig ligenden Kloster/ Borssholm genannt/ so nunmehro zu einer Land-Schule gewiedmet, nebenst 2. Knechten vorbey geritten/ in Willens daselbst im Wirthause zu futtern/ er an einen etwan einen Musqueten-Schuss von dem Wirts-Hause ligenden Hügel zu unterschiedenen malen ein klägliches Geschrey gehöret/ Kilian ist todt! Kilian ist todt! worauf er sich/ weil er gleichwol niemand im Felde gesehen/ nach dem Hügel gewendet/ und nebst seinen Knechten verspüret/ wie dieses Geschrey im Hügel wäre/ das er auch hierauf im Wirtshause nach genommenen Früh-Stücke dem Wirte erzehlet/ als zugleich die Magd eine Kanne Bier aufgesetzt/ und sobald sie solche Erzehlung angehöret/ mit kläglicher Stimme angefangen: Was? dass es GOTT erberme/ ist Kilian todt! und also fort auf den Hügel mit solchem Geschrey zugelauffen/ wohin ihr dann der Wirth gefolget/ und so viel vermerket, dass sie daselbst verschwunden/ auch niemals wieder zu Gesichte gekommen/ worauf er so ferner seinen Gesten erzehlet/ wie diese Magd gan-[p. 378]tzer vierzehen Jahr ihm gedienet/ und sich allezeit sonder die geringste Mutmassung dergleichen Ausgangs/ ehrlich verhalten hätte. Was duncket meinen Herren von dieser Sache? Ich weiss nicht/ was ich eigentlich darzu sagen sol/ antwortete der Herr Doctor/ ohne dass diese Geschichte mit dem Wunderhorn zu Oldenburg/ und denen aus der Erden in Engeland hervor gekrochenen grünen Kindern/ darvon Camdenus in seiner Beschreibung Engelands gedencket/ sehr überein kommet. . . .[35]

In another version[36] from Tyrol, the mysterious woman is said to be a visitor, known to be a forest-woman (*wildes Weib*), who comes every seven years. When she hears the message, "Tell Stizl at Wizl that Thorizl is dead," which is communicated to her without any questions about its intent, she says weeping, "If you had asked me concerning many things, I should have told you much." Here, accordingly, the creature is thought of as a friendly demon, whose association with the house is somewhat less intimate than was that of the maid or wife. The story is corrupt,

---

[35] Variant 1. I am indebted to Professor Hugo Hepding (of Giessen) for a transscript of this rare text. There are but three copies of Winckler's *Edelmann* in existence. The foregoing was taken from the volume owned by the University of Göttingen.

[36] Variant 83.

or has at least borrowed the response of the wild woman from some other tale in which it was more appropriately employed.[37] It seems obvious that we have here a minor variation of the story which has not become widely known. There is, so far as I know, but one other text[38] in which a similar combination occurs. It is defective, as appears from the fact that the *Fenken* have but one name, Wizi Wuzel, which accords well enough with the "Wizl" of the preceding tale. The story is as follows:

Two *Fenken* (masculine) and their sister were in the habit of warming themselves at a farmer's hearth. One day when the *Fangga* was sitting there alone her brother rushed in shouting, "Geh, Wizi Wuzel, der Wizi Wuzel ist gestorben!" Then she rose, saying:

> Hättet ihr mich mehr gefragt,
> So hätte ich euch mehr gesagt;
> Und wie man aus der "Schotta" (Molken)
> Hätte Wachs gemacht.

But not all the creatures in and about the house are friendly to the owner and his family. Inasmuch as he sees such hostile elves less frequently and has less to do with them the story of the death-message is more rarely associated with them. On some occasions the narration of the death surprises a thieving elf in the very act, a theme which seems favored by popular tradition in northern Germany and Denmark:

In Schleswig there was once an innkeeper whose stock of beer was always exhausted before it should be, without any assignable reason. Once he had gone to the city to purchase more and was just passing the Jagelberg, where there is a grave dating from heathen times (*Riesengrab*) on his return, when he heard some one wailing, "Pingel is dead!

---

[37] Cf. e.g., Baader, *Neue Volkssagen*, p. 272 (cited in Henne-am-Rhyn, *Die deutsche Volkssage²*, p. 335, No. 515); Zingerle, *Sagen aus Tirol²*, p. 54, No. 79, p. 64, Nos. 99, 100, cf. p. 602 (variant to No. 72), p. 603, No. 79, and p. 608, No. 99; Mannhardt, I, 112 and references; E. Meier, *Deutsche Sagen, Sitten und Gebräuche aus Schwaben*, Stuttgart, 1852, p. 45, No. 50; L. von Hörmann, *Mythologische Beiträge*, p. 7.

[38] Variant 93.

Pingel is dead!" After riding home in great fear and anxiety, he told what he had heard and just as he reached the words, "Pingel is dead!", a gnome came up from the cellar, shrieking:

  Alas, if Pingel is dead, if Pingel is dead,
  Then I have carried away enough beer.

He disappeared and beside the vat they found the jug in which he carried away the stolen beer for his sick comrade.[39]

The occurrence of the name Pingel is to be noted in another North German tale,[40] but in this there is no hint of stolen beer, and the non-appearance of this motive shows that the former one is a combination of two independent episodes. The story runs as follows:

 A messenger was sent to fetch an article needed at a wedding. His horse stopped in a copse and could not be induced to go on. Behind him he heard twice repeated, "Rider, segg Hahl, Pingel is dod!" The voice seemed to be that of a child. He went back and when he reported the news at the wedding, a wailing was heard among the guests. The sound moved toward the door and died away. But no one saw anything.

A similar tale[41] without mention of the wedding, is told near Schwerin in Mecklenburg. There the wailing in the mill lasted for a whole night. This story obviously belongs with the preceding ones, for here the name is Prigelken Pragelken. The variations in this group of tales, which is distinguished by the name Pingel and which is current only in the northernmost portion of Germany (Mecklenburg and Holstein), are, as we have seen, not inconsiderable and imply that the story has been in circulation for some time. Note further in another text "Prilling und Pralling"[42] and the occasional joining of the tale to the episode of the forgotten vessel.

 The justification which the Schleswig dwarfs might have alleged in their defense, that they were stealing for a sick

---

[39] Variant 25, cf. Variant 19.
[40] Variant 20.
[41] Variant 21.
[42] Variant 19.

comrade, cannot be advanced in the case of two Pomeranian dwarfs (*Öllerken*), who drop their jug on the appearance of a third with the news, "Têws! Purr Murr is dôd!"[43] Unfortunately the jug which they left behind in their flight was afterwards destroyed when the farm-house burned. As the story is told further north in Mecklenburg,[44] the dwarfs were in the habit of purchasing their beer—not of stealing it—and the silver can which the messenger dropped was long a prized object in the tavern-keeper's family. Another instance,[45] also from northern Germany, has already been cited in which the announcement of the message causes the unseen dwarf to drop the bag of dough which he was carrying off; and in a variant of the same tale[46] a voice instructs the astonished spectators to make three crosses on the dough as a protection against further losses of like nature. Gerhard considers this episode an important one, showing the persistence of the fertility-demon in the tradition. But from the parallels brought together by Grimm[47] it is clear that the notion of bread-stealing dwarfs is originally quite independent of our story, although later contaminations of the sort with which we are dealing are not infrequent. A parallel story, current in the Harz Mountains, may be mentioned as a further illustration of this rather unusual connecting of the demon with baking. The Harz story follows the ordinary type: the message is "Gödecke, Gödecke, sech mal vor Fredecken, sien Kind wolle starben!" To this Fredecke, a thieving gnome in the peasant Gödecke's house, replies, "Accursed Gödecke, why have you not put salt in the sour dough?" It does not appear that the ill-wishes of the gnome caused Gödecke any inconvenience.[48]

[43] Variant 3.
[44] Variant 21a.
[45] Variant 6.
[46] Variant 7.
[47] *Deutsche Mythologie*[4], I, 401, cf. III, 141.
[48] Variant 37.

Another story, which, like the foregoing, is said to be known in northern Germany (Mecklenburg) contains the same elements, but is rather pointless because the theft is omitted. It is particularly interesting for the introduction of a new episode explanatory of the dwarf's pot:

A wealthy peasant in Alt-Strelitz, the possessor of a fine herd of cows, was once visited by a dwarf, who asked for some milk in her pot. Since the cows had not yet been milked her brass pot was placed on the table with other vessels to be filled in its turn. While the little woman was waiting a smaller girl rushed into the room, crying, "Mother, come home quickly, little brother is just dead." Both ran out and were pursued out of the village by the school-children until they disappeared in a hill (Galgenberg). For a long time her jug was exhibited to guests as a rarity.[49]

A characteristic trait in these stories is the dropping of some object by the surprised elf; in some instances the pot or jug is preserved for a longer or shorter time, while in others, for instance the tale of the stolen dough, there is no momento of the dwarf's visit. It is clear enough that these northern German stories—and Danish parallels are abundant, too—are to be compared with those known both in northern and southern Germany in which the message calls forth an answer from a previously invisible house-haunting cobold or forest-woman. The notion of the auditory illusion which the latter embody has been enlarged and the incident acquires sharpness and distinctness by the mention of the forgotten vessel. These stories are merely accommodated to the belief, which is rather more widely current in northern Germany, that such creatures—not characteristically vegetation-demons, however—slily poach on the stores about them. And naturally enough, since local tradition is particularly familiar with this incident of the dwarf that drops a vessel in his precipitate flight, it is not surprising to find a considerable variety of combinations

[49] Variant 22.

of it with the episode of the death-message. Strackerjan collected two unimpeachable analogues from the folk in Oldenburg and one which, he thinks, may have been influenced by literary sources. The following narrative is typical and makes very clear the relation of the sounds heard to the auditory illusion. The whole recalls the activities of Wesley's *Poltergeist:*

> The *Erdmännchen* were in the habit of appearing at the farm Grashorn near Dingstede. They took what tidbits they could find and were particularly fond of beer. But the householder did not disturb them because, notwithstanding their petty thieveries, they brought prosperity to the farm and because, anyway, he was afraid to offend them. One night the *Erdmännchen* were heard moving about in the house as usual when suddenly a voice said, "Fehmöme is dead." Another answered, "If Fehmöme is dead, then my aunt (*Möhme*) is dead!" The uproar and thumping became louder for a time and finally all became silent. The *Erdmännchen* had gone away, but they left behind them a small pot of strange workmanship.[50]

In Strackerjan's second story[51] the message is brought by the farmer himself, who has heard it repeated as a queer sound which the inhabitants of a tavern could not understand.

This episode of the forgotten vessel and the thieving elves is also known in Denmark: Evald Tang Kristensen prints a score of examples, all of which differ slightly from one another. The following tale[52] will be a sufficient illustration of them all:

> A man who was bothered by dwarfs kept them away by drawing the sign of the cross on the beer-keg. One day when he forgot to put the sign on the keg, they tapped it and had drawn off two buckets of beer when one of them cried out, "Adder, have you heard that Madder is dead?" The news caused him to forget to replace the spigot, and the beer ran out on the floor.

[50] Variant 33.
[51] Variant 34.
[52] Variant 169.

The whole of this is capable, obviously enough, of explanation in terms of physical illusions, supplemented by the misfortune of the overflowing beer.[53] Occasionally, by a simple development (which appears, however, to be confined to Denmark), instead of stealing the beer the dwarfs by their presence prevent its being brewed, and only when the message is delivered and they have hastened off, does the beer ferment.[54] This last turn to the story, be it observed, is a very simple modification of the auditory illusion, and is obviously a developed form of the preceding tale. Certainly these stories have nothing of the demon of vegetation about them.

These stories are analogous to the previously mentioned narrative which Strackerjan suspected of having been influenced by some literary source. Inasmuch as the first episode resembles the stories of the beer-drinking dwarfs and can be paralleled in popular material, it seems reasonable to suppose that Strackerjan's tale represents in the main genuine folk-tradition, and it is so accepted by Elard Hugo Meyer in his *Mythologie der Germanen*. New is an episode similar to the "Luck of Edenhall,"[55] which is employed in a form awakening no suspicion. It is not, so far

[53] In other Danish tales (Variants 170–72) the message is "Bör (Skatte, Skotte, Asser) is fallen into the fire"; but the consequences are as before. One of these (Variant 170) contains the curious incident of the hill raised upon posts so that the passerby can see the company of dwarfs dancing beneath, an incident which will be illustrated and discussed later; cf. p. 42. The variation in the message, which can be paralleled, leads off, as we shall see, into a strange and entirely distinct tale; see below pp. 76 ff.

[54] Variants 175–76.

[55] Cf. A. Gröning, "Das Trinkhorn der Grafen von Oldenburg," *Am Urquell*, IV (1893), 208–9; *Müllenhoff, Sagen . . . aus Schleswig-Holstein*, p. 293, No. 402; T. Norlind, "Studier i svensk folklore," *Aarsskrift* (Lund Universitet), avd. 1, ny följd, VII (1911), 64 ff.; R. Bindel, *Kulturgeschichtliches aus den Schriften des 16. u. 17. Jahrh.*, Programm, Quakenbrück, 1909; cf. *Jahresberichte üb. neuere deutsche Literatur*, XIX–XX, 672.

as I know, elsewhere combined with our story. Strackerjan's tale[56] is as follows:

The *Erdmännchen* who dwelt in the interior of the Osenberge came at night to the inn Zum Streek, drew beer for themselves, and drank to their hearts' content, and left the amount of their reckoning in the drinking-vessels. Their queen, Fehmöme, offered a certain Count Otto a draught from her cup when he was lost in the mountains. He accepted and carried the cup away with him. She died from the exertion of running after him, and from sorrow over the loss. At the inn that night while the dwarfs were drinking as usual, the cry, "Fehmöme is dead" was heard and another voice sobbed, "If Fehmöme is dead, then my aunt (Möhme) is dead." The dwarfs were never seen after this event.

A curious modification of the story of the object dropped by the dwarf has been taken down in the valley of the Wupper, a tributary of the Rhein, and the southernmost point from which the combination of the death-message with the forgotten object has been reported. The version is said to be more than three hundred years old, but the authority for this is not given.

A tenant on monastery land sent his son Hänschen on an errand to the Bremersheide. While the boy was on his way home, he heard a pleasant voice calling his name and at the same moment he perceived a small bird which sang:

Say, Hänschen! As fresh and as red as you are,
Say, Hänschen! Tell Niesel, his wife is dead!

He hastened home where he found all assembled about the supper table and related his adventure. When he communicated the message a groan was heard at a vacant seat and a little knife fell on the table. A week later a dwarf appeared at the farmhouse and told how he had worked on the farmstead and eaten at the table. Shocked by the news, he had dropped his knife the return of which he now requested as a memento of his wife. Such knives, he explained, the dwarfs exchanged on their wedding days. He received his knife and was seen no more, but his activities continued to bring prosperity to the household.[57]

---

[56] Variant 35.
[57] Variant 40.

Or the story is adapted to the universal belief in changelings, as in this version from Carinthia:

> The peasant Posch was riding home one night on his white horse. While he was riding through the darkness of the night, some one cried to him:
> Posch,
> With your white horse,
> Tell your changeling,
> His brother Schedaweng is dead;
> Say that he is going to the church in the morning.
> The peasant rode home and next morning at breakfast told what he had experienced. The changeling behind the stove heard it, jumped down, and ran off.[58]

It is barely possible that there is some significance in the phrase "behind the stove," which also occurs in many of the Danish versions. The stove is of course the huge porcelain stove used throughout central Europe. I suspect that it may produce noises of all sorts and thus afford a physical basis for the illusion of the changeling which is heard "behind the stove."

It is not exactly clear why a changeling should leave one house when a like creature dies in another, but such an incident appears in one of the stories collected by Zingerle in Tyrol. Here, as in the preceding, who the peasant's informer was and what his concern in the matter may have been are left for us to guess. The story is as follows:

> Both at Posch's house in Mais and at Braiter's house in Kuens there were at the same time changelings. One evening an unknown man passed Posch's house and said, "Posch, with your crooked horse, tell my brother Dschedrawee that Kabeskopf (cabbage-head) is dead." On that very evening the child in Braiter's house died and after the announcement at the other house the second changeling disappeared without leaving a sign.[59]

[58] Variant 109.
[59] Variant 80.

The most cursory comparison of the two foregoing stories is sufficient to satisfy any one that they are derived from the same source; in no other way could the curious coincidence in regard to the name Posch and the other points of contact have arisen. Elsewhere Zingerle prints a tale[60] about the *Hollenleut,* who are said to be those of Adam's children whom he did not wish to acknowledge. In this the message is, "Prauss with your crooked horse, tell your maid Sagload, her mother is powder (*sic*) and is dead." The maid leaves in tears after she has given her mistress a ball of yarn, which, so long as its marvelous properties are not commented upon, will supply yarn. Of course the charm is ultimately broken.[61] And another Tyrolian version with an elaborate introduction telling how a peasant captured a water-elf (*Weiherjungfrau*) for a servant contains a message from her comrades in the pond similar to that employed in the changeling stories (viz., "Du Mann mit dem weissen Schimmel, sag' der Tille, der Mann sei gestorben"), and the incident of the endless ball of yarn.[62] It is a strange vegetation-myth which can be told with equal facility of changelings, of Eve's other children (*die ungleichen Kinder Eva*), and of a water-elf. Possibly it is a vegetation-myth because one version contains the name "cabbage-head!"

Inappropriately and clumsily enough our story and a familiar one about a changeling are combined in a Danish tale, apparently because both turn on the same general idea: the departure of a supernatural creature that haunts the house:

[60] Variant 98.

[61] The gift of such balls of yarn is a commonplace in these popular narratives, see, e.g., Zingerle, *Sagen aus Tirol*², p. 599, No. 53; p. 600, No. 63; p. 615, No. 168; R. Kühnau, *Schlesische Sagen*, II (1911), 177, No. 807; Freissauff, *Salzburger Volkssagen*, 1880, pp. 190–91; Jäcklin, *Volkstümliches aus Graubünden*, 1916, p. 124; Haupt, *Zs. f. d. Mythol.*, IV (1859), 222–3, No. 17.

[62] Variant 102.

As a man was passing Langhöj on his way home from the mill a dwarf came out of the hill and jumped on his wagon. When he arrived home it leapt down and took its place behind the porcelain stove. The neighbors suggested brewing in an eggshell to drive it away, and this did cause the creature some surprise, for it now spoke for the first time—but it did not leave, as all well-behaved changelings do. The man was passing Langhöj a second time when a voice called, "Greet Kukkeluris and tell him that Dawfeldt is dead!" When this was reported at home the dwarf disappeared to the satisfaction of man and wife.[63]

This example like the preceding one is instructive as showing the power of our story to attract unrelated incidents to itself. The cobold, which, as here, leaves when it receives a new coat is a commonplace[64] in popular literature:

A peasant at Nauders in Tyrol enjoyed prosperity because a *Nörkele* lived in the household. The *Nörkele* took delight in tying cattle together and in similar pranks; once it saw eggshells lying on the hearth and remarked, "O what pretty dishes and bowls." When the peasant laid some clothing on the hearth it departed, going to another farm where there was a *Nörklweibl*, to whom it brought the news, "Stûze Mûze, di rauche Rintn is gstorbn." Both disappeared.[65]

A rare and unusually terrifying form of the story in which the traveler himself is the cause of the death and is the bearer of the news to an avenger has been taken down by Müllenhoff in Schleswig-Holstein:

A man riding past a mountain in the evening noticed that it was raised on pillars and that the dwarfs (Bergleute) were dancing under it. He threw his pocket-knife into the company and a dancer fell dead. As he rode swiftly homeward a voice cried after him, "Tell Find the little Kind is dead." At the supper-table a man servant listened attentively to the narration of the incident and when the message was repeated, seized a large bread-knife and drove it into his master's breast. Then the murderer disappeared.[66]

[63] Variant 222.
[64] Cf. Feilberg, *Zs. d. Ver. f. Volksk.*, VIII (1898), 143 ff.
[65] Variant 49.
[66] Variant 27.

The strange picture of the mountain resting on pillars so that the passer-by can see into the interior is not unfamiliar in Norse saga and has mythological associations of the greatest interest.[67] The notion of the dead feasting in the hill seems to fall somewhere between the idea of the continued residence of the dead in the grave and the highly elaborated Viking myth of Valhalla. This bit of ancient folk-belief about the dead and what sounds like a *crime passionel* are joined with the mysterious message of death to form a shocking little tale.

This North German (or more strictly Danish) tale, although it may have been a little embellished, is the best example of a form which is also preserved, but less perfectly, in two Danish stories. The distinguished Danish folklorist, Evald Tang Kristensen, prints nearly seventy instances of our story, but only two of his collection are of this form. Inasmuch as Müllenhoff's tale stands equally alone among as many German variants, one can say with a confidence somewhat rare in matters of this kind that we are dealing with a rather unusual form. The Danish stories are very brief:

There was once a dwarf in Viuf and no one knew he was there. The man who lived on Hans Nielsen's farm in Viuf told his servant one day to go to the mill. When he came to the hill on the mill-road, a dwarf came out and disappeared down a hole in the hill. The fellow took a few stones and threw them down the hole. Then the dwarf appeared again and said: "Tell Finndkind that little Kee is dead." The fellow had killed one of the dwarf's children. When he came home in the evening he told what he had done and then the "hill-man" who was on Hans Nielsen's farm departed, going into the hill by night, but before he went he cut the man's throat.[68]

[67] The classical parallel to this scene is the eleventh chapter of the old and trustworthy *Erbyggjasaga;* for further parallels see *Njalssaga,* ch. 14, 139; Vigfusson and Powell, *Corpus Poeticum Boreale,* I, 415, and the handbooks on Germanic mythology. It is still a part of current Danish folk-belief; cf. Kristensen, *Danske Sagn,* Aarhus, 1892, I, 198 ff., §47, Höje på pæle og dands derinde, Nos. 726–69.

[68] Variant 220.

The second story is even shorter:

> There is a hill in Viuf mark called Femhöje. A man who was driving to Don's mill, passed it, and there was dancing down in the hill. He threw a stone down. Then a dwarf came up and said, "Tell Finndke that Lill is dead."[69]

It is clear from the regularity with which the name Find occurs in these particular stories that all of them are derived from a common source, to which this fragment—I give it entire—must belong: "A dwarf leaps on the farmer's wagon, "Tell Find his little Rosenkind is dead."[70] More important than the fact that the versions containing these characteristic names can be traced back to a common source is the observations that in them the gnomes are conceived as the souls of the dead, not vegetation-demons.

Retribution also overtook a Bavarian man-servant who used his alpenstock to kill an elf milking his cow in spite of the local belief that such creatures bring prosperity and should not be injured. The man went crazy after the murder, and on the following evening he heard a voice crying, "Up with all nine kingdoms! Elfe is dead!" and threw himself into a lake.[71] The tale has no close parallels and is a very curious modification of those that we have seen. Certainly there is no reason to relate it to any myth of Frô, as some have done.[72] There is a remote parallel to a part of the story in a collection of Tyrolese legends, which shows that the Bavarian tale is really a combination of two episodes. The "Donandel," we are told, are mountain demons which love cattle; they drive the animals off precipitous slopes to safe grazing places and care for them in their stalls in winter. One man could not endure the sight of a "Donandel," and struck the little fellow down

---

[69] Variant 221.
[70] Variant 203.
[71] Variant 50.
[72] J. W. Wolf, *Beiträge*, II, 280.

from his perch between a cow's horns. The elf rose uninjured and pronounced a curse on the mountain meadow: that it should lose its grass and water. The curse was fulfilled, and but one-fifth as many cattle can graze on "Grünalpe" as before. No punishment seems to have been inflicted on the wrong-doer.[73]

A heterogeneous and not particularly happy compounding of at least three stories, one of them being the Pan tale, is printed by Kuhn in his *Sagen aus Westfalen:*

> A count continued his relations with a dwarf-woman until his wife learned that they were meeting in the Mömkenloch. She surprised them together, and the count promised her that he would not visit the dwarf again. There followed some persecution of the count by the dwarfs, and on one occasion a good deal of property was stolen from the castle. Finally they departed, and a voice was heard crying, "Up, up, Prinz, Prinzerlenz, Prinz is dead." Later in the same night a man came to the ferryman asking him to have his boat in readiness for passengers. Four times he crossed the river without seeing his freight, which, nonetheless, caused the boat to sink low in the water. After the last trip his employer ordered him to look at the meadow, where he could now see the multitude he had transported. He was also informed that his pay was in the bottom of the boat, but, when he found only horsedung there, he threw it out in vexation. On the morrow, however, what had stuck to his shoe had turned to gold.[74]

The looseness of the junctures is quite apparent: the story of the count's jealous wife has nothing to do with the events that follow. It is moreover a familiar enough story in independent form.[75] This episode of invisible ship-

---

[73] Freissauff, *Salzburger Sagen*, pp. 221–23.

[74] Variant 36.

[75] See Kuhn, *Sagen aus Westfalen*, I, 159–60, No. 165 (and references), which is reprinted in O. Schell, *Bergische Sagen*, pp. 138–39, No. 5 (with further references, p. 577). The woman according to the analogues, said nothing bitter to her supernatural rival, but, picking up her hair, remarked only, "God protect your beautiful hair." Cf. E. H. Meyer, *Mythologie der Germanen*, 1903, p. 188; Henne-am-Rhyn,

loads of dwarfs (souls) is an early bit of Germanic folklore, vouched for by Procopius (IV.20), who relates that it was believed that the souls were ferried every night across to Britain.[76] This combination is important for us because it makes perfectly clear that the actors are here conceived as dwarfs, the souls of the dead. A similar conclusion could also be arrived at by considering the preceding tale about the dwarfs dancing in the hollow hill. Surely the story which is attached to such creatures bears no marks of being inherently a vegetation-myth.

This combination for the stories of the ferrying of the souls and of the message of death occurs in other tales than the one just cited. A typical example is as follows:

A little man asked a ferryman on the Ems to ferry him across in a large barge used for four-horse wagons. As the ferryman was about to push off he was commanded to wait for an order to do so, and after a long delay the order was given. The boat sank low in the water, although only the little man was to be seen. On the other side he asked what the charge was and was told a *Stüber* apiece. The company, some

Die deutsche Volkssage[2], p. 279, No. 430; Mannhardt, *Wald- und Feldkulte*, I, 102; Laistner, *Rätsel der Sphinx*, I, 146–53; Ranke, *Die deutschen Volkssagen*, I, 183, cf. p. 282; Panzer, *Bayerische Sagen und Bräuche*, I, 13; Grimm, *Deutsche Sagen*, No. 71; Vernaleken, *Alpensagen*, 1858, pp. 226–27, No. 155; Freissauff, *Salzburger Sagen*, Vienna, 1880, pp. 131–33; J. Krainz, *Mythen und Sagen aus dem steirischen Hochlande*, Bruck a.d. Mur, 1880, p. 394, No. 300; P. Zaunert, *Deutsche Natursagen, Erste Reihe*, Jena, 1921, pp. 31, 74–75, 137–38. In a variant form of the story the wife cuts off the woman's hair; see Freissauff, pp. 190–91, 191–92, 197.

[76] Kuhn and Schwartz, *Norddeutsche Sagen*, p. 111, No. 126, 5; p. 242, No. 270, 1, (and p. 499); p. 259, No. 291; Bartsch, *Sagen aus Mecklenburg*, I, 57, No. 73; p. 58, No. 74; Ranke, *Die deutschen Volkssagen*, IV, pp. 145 ff.; Böckel, *Die deutsche Volkssage*, p. 37; Wucke, *Sagen der mittleren Werra*, Salzungen, 1864, I, 117, 121; O. Schell, *Bergische Sagen*, Elberfeld, 1897, p. 449, No. 57 (cf. p. 598), p. 480, No. 33 (cf. p. 600 and references); P. Zaunert, *Deutsche Natursagen*, I (Jena, 1921), pp. 52–54, 139–40; Sébillot, *Folklore de France*, II, 148 ff.; Feilberg, *Zs. des Ver. f. Volkskunde*, VIII (1898), 276, n. 5; Grimm, *Deutsche Mythologie*,[4] p. 694; Meiche, *Sagenbuch des Königreichs Sachsen*, pp. 325–26, No. 429; Kühnau, *Schlesische Sagen*, II (1911), p. 114, No. 755, 6; p. 115, No. 755, 7; p. 116, No. 755, 8; E. T. Kristensen, *Danske Sagn*, I, 423 ff., Nos. 1363 ff.; A. Haas, *Blätter f. pomm. Volkskunde*, X (1902), "Zwergsagen, No. 5"; Andree, *Am Urquell*, IV (1893), 226–7. Cf. Herzog, *Schweizersagen*[2], II, 144–45, No. 133.

declare, cried, "The King is dead, the king is dead! Now we must leave."[77]

And a queer transmogrification of the story of the departing elves as it is combined with our story is offered in Switzerland as an explanation for the doom of a particular Wild Huntsman[78] and for the departure of the elves:

> A drunken Piedmontese carrier driving over a pass with his load of Italian wine rode down a narrow road where it was difficult to give room to those coming up. At this place he slashed a dwarf with his whip instead of turning out for him. The injured man cried aloud until all the dwarfs in the valley had collected, and then they shouted, "Run, run, Rebärben; father is about to die." Then they left the countryside and for three days and three nights they were heard sobbing, as they crossed the Grimsel pass. The driver and his horses went on. The lead-horse fell over a precipice and dragged the others with the wagon after it, and the driver, seeing that all was lost, threw himself into the abyss. But death did not expiate his crime, for he must drive on shouting, shrieking, and cracking his whip until Judgment Day.[79]

In Bavaria our story is brought, although loosely, into some sort of connection with another old mythical notion: the belief that a king in the Untersberg awaits the hour of his country's need. The story is as follows:

> In Bildenau a *Bergmanl* and his wife were employed by a peasant. Once when the man-servant was working in the field, the woman left her washing and ran to her husband, crying, "Jacob, come quickly, we must go to Untersberg, King Carl is dead!"[80]

In Alpenburg's collection of tales from Tyrol the story is very clearly assimilated to the belief in vegetation-demons, and this instance with its immediate parallels, which form a distinct and easily recognizable group, is therefore one of the chief supports of Mannhardt's interpretation. The

---
[77] Variant 8.
[78] For parallels to this part of the story see Kohlrusch, *Schweizerisches Sagenbuch*, p. 41, No. 11 and pp. 76–77, No. 37.
[79] Variant 70.
[80] Variant 46.

members of this group also often fall into a well represented class, that of the maid who is called away from the household by the news of death. The example which Mannhardt selects as a starting-point is as follows:

An unknown maid with gigantic strength in service with a peasant in Flies knew and wished to know nothing about Christianity. Once the peasant was coming home over the Pillerberg from Imstermarkt and as he passed through the Bannwald, he heard all at once from the depths of the forest a loud, unfamiliar voice cry out, "Yoke-bearer (*Jochträger*), yoke-bearer, tell Stutzamutza, Hoachrinta is dead." And then all was silent again. The peasant was bearing over his shoulder the yokes of the oxen he had sold. Perspiring with fear he came home and told his experience to his wife and the maid. The latter jumped up, shrieking, "Mother, mother!" and disappeared in the direction of the Bannwald. The report soon became current that she was living in the forest and continuing the activities of her mother, the stealing and devouring of little children.[81]

Another version, published by Alpenburg, makes clearer, if need be, the significance attached to the queer names in the message; but Mannhardt questions for some reason its authenticity. In view of the parallels there seems to be no sufficient reason to suspect it. Here it is:

Between Landeck and Ladis on the right bank of the Inn lies the notorious forest of the wild women (*Fanggen*) in the valley of the Urgen. A herdsman was looking for one of his lost cattle there when he found a child completely covered with hair. He took her home, reared her, and she became a maid in the household. She learned to talk but would never listen to anything religious and was most at home in the forest. Once two men were walking past the forest where she had been found and they heard in the pines a rough, commanding voice cry, "Tell Stutzfärche (the fir), Rohrinde (rough bark)[82] has been felled and is dead." The men were amazed and did not know how to explain the words. One of them, a friend of the herdsman with whom the maid was staying, told the incident in such a loud voice that she heard it from

---

[81] Variant 87.

[82] Rochholz (*Schweizersagen*, I, 346) would etymologize this as "die Rêrende," i.e., the wailing one, the woman called away (*Abberufende* [sic]).

an adjoining room. Then she began to weep and cried out, while running to the forest where she had been found. She was never seen again. Just at that time a few of the old trees had been felled.[83]

In his important collection of traditions from Tyrol Zingerle tells a similar story with the characteristic names. Although the peasant cannot induce Stutzamutza to remain she tells him how to keep the prosperity which she has brought to the household. Her instructions are, "If you wish to be prosperous in your management, then love and treat well the 'hairy worm.'" The farmer guesses rightly that she means the black cat on the hearth. In a variant from Findels in the same region the cat is called the "hairy foot," and the further injunction to keep the hearth clean is added.[85] The queer leave-taking appears only in the southern German and Tyrolese stories; a third instance and the last that I have noted gives the forest-woman's (Hitte Hatte's) words as follows: "Ist der Jordan tot, so bin ich froh! Haltet den haarigen Hausworm wohl und habt Glück zum Vieh!"[86] The relation between the maid, who is unquestionably a forest-woman, a species of vegetation-demon, and the cat is not obvious. In this connection Mannhardt's remark that Stutzamutza means "Stutzkatze" seems significant,[87] but unfortunately this interpretation of the name is not uncontested: Rochholz[88] observes that *Mückenstutz*, a dwarf's name, seems to have reference to the association of dwarfs and butterflies (cf. Mücke, "midge"). In some of these tales the names, e.g., Mao, Mamao, are obviously chosen to simulate mewing.[89] Fur-

[83] Variant 88.
[84] Variant 99.
[85] Variant 104.
[86] Variant 52.
[87] The name Stutzimutzi is applied to a Venedigerfräulein in Sepp, *Sagenschatz*, p. 35. Such creatures are related to the witch rather than to the forest-woman; the name seems to have been transferred from its true use.
[88] *Schweizersagen*, I, 346–47.
[89] Variant 94.

thermore, a large group of tales have, as we shall see, cats as actors.

Although the following Swabian version is obviously defective, it is not without interest. Signs of corruption also appear, it will be recalled, in a variant of this type from Baden, and other deviations from what seems to have been the original form of the story have already been mentioned. The fact that the story is more perfectly preserved in this form in and about Tyrol seems to indicate that it originated there and the farther it wandered from that region the less perfectly it was understood. The Swabian tale is especially interesting because of its very clear intimation of the noises of the forest:

> A man working in a field near a forest caught a *Holzweiblein*. The next day he went out again to the forest, where another *Holzweiblein* called to him from a tree, "Hey! man, yoke-bearer (*Jochträger*), is Staunzen Maunzen at home, is she well?" Filled with fear, he ran home again.[90]

An even clearer example which hints at an auditory illusion as its basis is the following Swiss tale:

> The dwarfs often used to come to help the mowers and the herdsmen on the Great Scheidegg. They came either from the upper glacier or from that of the Scheidegg. Once when the people were haying there, they heard from the Scheidegg the cry: "Ju lo lo! Muggistutz is dead!" He had been the leader of the dwarfs. Since then they come no more.[91]

Rochholz[92] notes that Johannes Leopold Cyswat, who has been called the first Swiss folk-lorist, remarks that the bittern was locally known in Lucerne as "Rohrind" or "Mosskuh" and he interprets these names as reminiscent

[90] Variant 64.
[91] Variant 73a. Gerhard considers important the fact that some of these stories thus emphasize the existence of a leader. The preceding one he does not know, but he cites an obviously corrupted and Christianized version, "Stutzi Mutzi! Morgen müssen wir zur Kirche gehen, weil der Obriste gestorben ist!" (Variant 51; reprinted in Freissauff, p. 212); cf. *Wiener Stud.*, XXXVII (1915), 347, n. 1.
[92] *Schweizersagen*, I, 346 citing *Beschreibung des Vierwaldstätter Sees*, 1661, p. 80.

of those familiar to us and therefore as implying the existence of this special form of the tale in the early years of the seventeenth century.

This group of variants is perhaps sufficiently represented by the examples that have been given. It is particularly frequent in collections of tales from Tyrol,[93] but versions are known from southern Bavaria, Baden, and Swabia.[94] The tale from Baden,[95] which has already been cited in another connection, is thus shown to belong to this group, for it contains the characteristic name "Jochträger." In a version from Tyrol[96] the name "Mon-jochträger" is erroneously transferred to the chief of the forest-men ("wilde Männer"), who is represented as ordering Stutza-Mutza to return home now that her mother is dead. Since a terrible howling and wailing followed her disappearance the folk suppose that she was torn to bits. The story is obviously confused, and therefore cannot be used to establish the thesis that there was a hierarchy among the "wilde Leute." Another tale,[97] taken down in the valley of the Inn, keeps only the name "Jochträger" and changes the others to "Florinde" and "Heringingele," jingling names which were certainly suggested by "Rohrinde." According to this tale, a giant hanged Florinde to a tree after she had fled from the inn on hearing the news of the death. These last two stories have taken up and put to use the traditional hostility of these wild men for the forest-women, a hostility which appears also in the Tyrolese myths of the Wild Hunt and elsewhere.

Henne-am-Rhyn cites these names, Stutza-Mutza and Rohrinde, as occurring in Switzerland and Bohemia, but

[93] Variants 74–78, 84, 87, 88, 90, 99, 103, 104.
[94] Variants 48–49, 63, 66.
[95] Variant 66; see above, p. 29.
[96] Variant 98.
[97] Variant 104.

gives no references to his sources.[98] Reiser prints a handful of tales of this type from the Bavarian Allgäu, which show peculiar and instructive modifications in the names, e.g., Jochträger, Stuzze Maruzze, Schalingge;[99] Stuzzemuzz, Ahudlamuz;[100] Jochträger, Gstutzte Mutz, Loringg;[101] Stuzze Muzz, Sala Wenzel;[102] Studese Muzz;[103] and as an example of still greater alteration: Tschudre Mudre, Harischka.[104] Forms in *-ing* are presumably corruptions of *-rinde*, although I would not go so far as Panzer[105] and compare the name and figure with the Old Norse Rinda. Examples of this sort are: Maringga, Maringger;[106] Ringgede Bingge, Frau Marie Ringge.[107] It is clear that when the names had lost their original meaning to the folk, they were felt merely as a jingle and a forgotten name could be modelled after one which was remembered, e.g., Maringga, Maringger. For one pair of names used in the Allgäu I have no explanation; it is Kolumban, Tanne Hans.[108]

In Rhaetia and Vorarlberg our story is told as an explanation of the unusual situation of a large boulder. According to the narrator, the departing maid threw a large rock, which many men could not have moved, into an abyss. The message which was brought to her varies somewhat from the familiar form: "Jochträger, sag der Rûchrinden: Gika-

[98] For Switzerland I may cite Variants 67, 73a, and the discussion above, p. 49.
[99] Variant 53.
[100] Variant 54.
[101] Variant 55.
[102] Variant 59.
[103] Variant 61; the story is corrupt in other regards.
[104] Variant 58.
[105] *Bayerische Sagen und Bräuche*, II, 464, cf. p. 570.
[106] Variant 56.
[107] Variant 57.
[108] Variant 61. Some Tyrolese tales have names which cannot be easily explained as mutilations of the familiar names, e.g., "Bubo! der Talitz ist gestorben! (Variant 113); "Mensch mit deiner Last! Sag' der Braunabis in der Brandstatt, der Vater Gabis ist todt! (Variant 114); "Waldadl ist todt!" (Variant 115).

Gäki sei todt auf Hungerhorn."[109] This form of the message is not to be rejected as a mishearing of the narrator, for there is a parallel to it in Canton Graubünden: "Jochträger, sag der Ruchrinden, Gücki Gäcki auf Hungerhorn sei todt!"[110]

No one will be inclined, I think, to question the correctness of Mannhardt's opinion[111] that all these varying names can be traced back to a single, perhaps not very remote source which possessed the names Jochträger, Rauchrinde (or Hochrinde), and Stutzamutza.

In a few of the Allgäu tales preserving the characteristic names the story exhibits a striking and probably significant resemblance to some of the Danish variants. Compare the following example:

> Once a peasant of Kappel (near Schatwald) sold a pair of oxen and was carrying home the yoke. As he came to Staiger Kirchweg he heard a voice call, "Jochträger, tell Gstutzte Mutz, Loringg is dead!" When he told this at home there was a wailing and moaning and shrieking behind the stove that was sad to hear, and yet no one saw anything at all.[112]

The similarity to the Danish tales implies pretty clearly that this form is nearer the primitive original than the elaborated tales. Both the Danish tales and those from the mountains of southern Germany show every evidence of being products of the soil with a fairly long antecedent history. There is pretty clearly no probability of the influence of one version upon the other. If we were dealing with linguistic instead of narrative material, there could be no reasonable doubt of the priority of the form common to Denmark and the south. But this common form is obviously based upon an auditory illusion and not upon a nature-myth.

[109] Variant 72.
[110] Variant 67.
[111] I, 91, n. 2.
[112] Variant 55; cf. Variant 60.

It may have seemed that southern Germany and Tyrol knew only the story with the names Stutzamutza and Rohrinde. There are, however, some scattering instances with names which cannot be derived from those characteristic of that story, and there is, furthermore, evidence of the existence of an independent group, distinguished by special names for the actors, which is found only in the Italian Tyrol. This group, of which three or four instances have been printed, may be recognized by the use of the name "Taratong" or "Tarandone." Among several versions of the story of the housemaid (or wife) who must leave when her name is disclosed, there is one[113] in which she leaves when a powerful voice calls from the mountain, "Gei gei! Taratta, chè Taratong l'è mort." Schneller took down another variant[114] in the same region. As parallel to this I might cite a Styrian tale[115] in which a maid who had been friendly with the "forest-women" leaves on hearing the message, "Mirzl, die Toni is g'storb'n."[116] This group of stories is insignificant in numbers, displays no interesting variations, and is noteworthy only because it contains the southernmost instances of the story, and among them a few in Italian.

A curious tale has been taken down in Switzerland in which there appear obvious reminiscences of the belief in the ghostly funeral which is a warning of an actual funeral. The folk near Freiburg in Switzerland tell the following tale:

Old Hans Aeby and his wife Appolonia lived in a lonely hut on the edge of a forest. One winter night he heard a clear voice cry, "Hans Aeby, sag' dem Appele, d'Appela sei todt!" After these words he heard a soft rustling in the room and a scarcely audible sobbing. The cry was repeated at midnight and Hans sprang from his bed and ran to the

[113] Variant 92.
[114] Variant 96.
[115] Variant 111.
[116] Toni for Antonia is possibly a reminiscence of Tarandone.

window. He saw without a troop of dwarfs passing over the snow-covered meadow. Some were dressed in black, others bore flaming torches, and the women were dressed in mourning clothes. They were carrying a coffin much too heavy for their strength. Wailing, they disappeared in the forest. The next day a messenger came to bring the news that Hans' wife's mother had died from apoplexy.[117]

In Saxony and Bohemia[118] the story has been worked into an elaborate tale of a dwarf-wedding, although not without some expense to the original anecdote:

In Dittersbach (near Friedland in Bohemia) a dwarf visited a woman in childbed to ask permission to use her room for a banquet. She assented to the request and watched the feasting with great enjoyment. But the dancing had scarcely begun when a newcomer rushed in, clasped his hands over his head, and cried out in a sorrowful voice:

O grosse Noth, O grosse Noth,
Die alte Mutter Pumpe ist todt.

The merrymakers at once took flight, each one bearing with him some part of the equipment of the feast. Only the creature who had first asked for the use of the room remained; he thanked his hostess for her kindness, explaining that the sudden death of an ancestress had caused them all great sorrow and anxiety and that they might now become very wretched. He left three gifts, a golden ring, a silver cup, and a roll of wheaten bread, which he declared to be of the greatest importance, for so long as all three gifts are in the family's possession, it will be prosperous, respected, and rich. The cup and the loaf were inclosed in the stone walls of a tower and the ring was thenceforth worn continually by the wife of the eldest son of the house. When, after some generations, the ring was lost, the tower was split by a stroke of lightning and the remaining gifts were destroyed. When all the gifts had vanished the good fortune of the family ceased.

That a combination exists here is, of course, obvious and it is hardly necessary to point out that the tale of the three fortune-bringing talismans has been taken down in Pomerania and elsewhere quite independently of our story.[119]

[117] Variant 72.
[118] Variant 45.
[119] Grässe, *Sagenbuch des Königreichs Sachsen*, 1855, pp. 269–70, No. 374 (cf. p. 578); Jahn, *Volkssagen aus Pommern*², 1890, pp. 81–2, No. 100; J. W. Wolf, *Bei-*

The version printed by the brothers Grimm, is, although it dates from the early years of the eighteenth century (1719), pretty certainly confused, for the message is construed as having a favorable bearing. While the company of dwarfs was seated at dinner, Lady Charlotte Elizabeth of Orleans relates, a *Weibchen* ran in, crying:

> Gottlob und Dank, wir sind aus grosser Not,
> Denn die alte Schump ist tot.[120]

We may suppose, however, that the form *Schump* is more original than *Pump*, for the former occurs in a Middle High German tale (which has nothing to do with this one).[121]

A similar vague and unexplained anxiety takes possession of the dwarfs in a tale from Schleswig-Holstein, for they cry

> If Eisch is dead, if Eisch is dead,
> Then we are all in great danger.[122]

In other particulars this story accords with the familiar North German tale of the beer-stealing dwarfs who leave their cup behind. Gerhard, who considers (p. 39) this trait an ancient and important one, reminiscent of the sadness which once expressed itself in an annual, ceremonial bewailing of the death of the demon of vegetation, compares further the cries of the "wild women" in Tyrol on the eve of their flight:

träge zur deutschen Mythologie, II, 316; Gander, *Niederlausitzer Volkssagen*, Berlin, 1894, pp. 47–48, No. 121, cf. p. 156; Meiche, *Sagenbuch des Königreichs Sachsen*, 1903, pp. 320–21, No. 423; Grimm, *Deutsche Sagen*, Nos. 69, 71 and notes; Haupt, *Zs. f. d. Mythol.*, IV (1859), 214, No. 3; cf. Müllenhoff, *Sagen . . . aus Schleswig-Holstein*, pp. 327 ff., No. 443, and p. 604. The request to use the room for a dwarf's wedding is found in other stories; see Grimm, *Deutsche Sagen*, Nos. 31, 35, 41; Golther, *Handbuch der deutschen Mythologie*, p. 136. Cf. Czechenberz, "Die Wöchnerin und die Zwerge," *Zs. f. österr. Vk.*, X (1903), 140, No. 11.

[120] Variant 43.

[121] See Grimm, *Deutsche Mythologie*, I, 375 n. There may be a reminiscence of the favorable outcome of this tale in the rhyme from the Kuhländchen (Moravia) which is quoted by Grimm (*Deutsche Mythologie*,[4] III, 479).

[122] Variant 24.

Rune (fem.) and Tuit (masc.) are dead,
We shall die tomorrow.[123]

But if such cries of departing demons are to be admitted to the discussion it would become interminable.[124] It seems rather hard to believe that a detail of the original story so significant for Gerhard's interpretation would be thus preserved in an obscure trait in a highly elaborated and artificial form of the story. And the existence of a similar tale among the aborigines of South America about the time of the conquest speaks very strongly against his interpretation. "The hapiñuñu, or bosom-clutching spirits, who were believed to have been the original inhabitants of the Peruvian valleys, were," we are told, "forcibly expelled by the early human inhabitants, immigrants from the country of the Guaycurus. When the ancestors of the Incas arrived in the sierra 'from beyond Potosi'—that is, from the Gran Chaco,—these spirits, according to a fragment of an ancient song which has been preserved by an Indian writer, disappeared with terrible cries, saying:

'We are conquered! We are conquered!
Alas, for I lose my lands.'"[125]

A further striking and significant narrative, which makes use of the cries of mourning demons, has been brought to my attention by Professor Hepding (of Giessen). This, the only modern Greek tale in any way comparable with

[123] See also Mannhardt, I, 93, n.; I. V. Zingerle, *Sagen, Märchen . . . aus Tirol*, 1859, p. 32, No. 42; I. V. Zingerle, Sagen aus Tirol², pp. 45-6, No. 69, cf. p. 601; Henne-am-Rhyn, *Die deutsche Volkssage*,² p. 140, No. 271; Kühnau, *Schlesische Sagen*, II, 66-67, No. 732; Meiche, *Sagenbuch des Königreichs Sachsen*, p. 351, No. 459; Jegerlehner, *Sagen und Märchen aus dem Oberwallis*, 1913, pp. 193-94, No. 87.

[124] A few instances are collected in Rochholz, *Schweizersagen*, I, 348, cf. p. 338. See also Herzog, *Schweizersagen*, 1871, p. 40, No. 40; p. 41, No. 41; p. 150, No. 154; Grimm, *Deutsche Mythologie*, I, 401.

[125] Hartland, *Ritual and Belief*, New York, 1914, p. 178 quoting from Payne, *History of the New World called America*, Oxford, 1892-99, I, 391, who cites Lozano, *Desc. Chorographica de Gran Chaco*, 1733, p. 71.

the texts under consideration, is found in Polites' great storehouse of contemporary traditions, Μελέται περὶ τοῦ βιοῦ καὶ τῆς γλώσσης τοῦ ἑλλένικοῦ λαοῦ : παραδόσεις (Athens, 1904, I, 408, No. 694). The difficulty of the Cretan dialect in which the story was taken down has prevented me from giving a complete, literal translation. Because of the importance of this version I give below a translation in which, fortunately, no essential detail is obscure. For substantial assistance in reading the text I am indebted to Professor Thomas S. Duncan. It is as follows:

. . . how two men had gone up to rather high hills where wild animals have their homes. They sat all night in the moonlight in a . . .(?) that they might catch game. There they heard a great noise, and they hoped that (the noise makers) might be men that they might heap snow upon them because they were taking it to Chania. As soon as they went nearer, they heard the sound of violins and harps and music set to words. They had never heard such music before. For this reason they knew that they were not men but were a company of spirits. They observe them and then withdraw a short space from the place where they had been sitting, in the dress of a soothsayer, and some with tunes unaccompanied by words and others with tunes accompanied by the words. And they showed that they were women and men, on foot and astride horses, a wedding (?) company. The men were white like doves, the women very beautiful, like the rays of the sun. And they looked at and carried a bridegroom (?) even as they carry the body of a dead man.

Meanwhile the company declare that they will pelt with sand those [that are carrying the bridegroom (?)] till they fall before them. They had also a well-known song, and sang as follows:

> Strike our sister (in-law):
> Let us throw her,
> Our maiden sister (in-law)
> From the headland (?),
> Our sister, an only child.

Thus they declare, and they rush upon her at once and pelt her with sand. Thereupon the others cried out, those in front, with one voice, "What is it? [What is the matter?]" Those in the rear answer, "They have blinded our brother (-in-law)! They have blinded our brother (-in-law)!" And they wept and cried and fled.

On the island of Guernsey our story is associated with what seems to be a much corrupted and even more familiar tale:

A man (who is apparently supernatural) calls a woman away from her house one night and she is gone until morning. When she returns she brings a little baby with her, to whom she gives the name Colin. She rears him and when he is 15 years of age, the minister takes him into his house as a servant. Some time later the minister is returning at night past a stone which is called "Le Roc du Coq Chantant" in the neighborhood, when he hears a voice crying, "Jean Dumaresq! Jean Dumaresq!" over and and over again. When he stops the cries cease and he hears the message, "Tell little Colin that big Colin is dead!" When the boy hears the news he is unwilling to wait for his wages and, after saying farewell to his foster-mother, disappears forever.[126]

The connection between the introductory episode, which recalls the incident of the woman called to assist a dwarf or fairy-woman in her hour of need, and our story is very loose, and the style of the whole smacks of literature rather than the folk. The most significant feature for us in this tale is, however, not the combination of the two elements, but the name of the rock where the minister hears the message. That name, Le Roc du Coq Chantant, implies pretty clearly that the spot was known and named for its auditory illusions.

Sir Edgar MacCulloch, whilom Bailiff of the Island of Guernsey, tells the same story with the same names, but without the stupid introductory episode.[127] He follows it with another and a quite different one in which Le Grand Colin and Le Petit Colin appear as honest and industrious elves. Our story has also, he remarks, been printed and

[126] Variant 240.
[127] Variant 241.

discussed in a French paper from which he extracts a third version[128] current in Guernsey with the explanatory observation that Colin was a troll or goblin in the form of a cat or monkey who was persecuted by his master. In all of these examples it should be particularly noticed that the scene is "La Roque où le Coq Chante" or "Le Roc du Coq Chantant."

Perhaps the strangest employment of this message of death is as an omen as in the fifty-third and following chapters of the Saga of Olaf Tryggvason:

> Earl Hakon accompanied by one thrall, Kark, having fled before King Olaf, slept for a night in a hole now called the Earl's Hole, and on awakening told his companion his dream,—that a black threatening man had come into the hole, and was angry that people had entered it, and had said, "Ulle is dead." The earl said that his son Erlend must be killed. The black man appeared to Kark when he fell asleep a second time and bade him tell the earl that all the sounds are closed. This the earl thought betokened a short life for him, and the two went on to seek concealment at the house of Thora, the earl's only friend in the valley. She hid them beneath the pig-stye. Olaf came thither searching for the earl and in a loud voice promised rewards and honors to the man who should kill him. Kark heard all this and changed color,—but assured Hakon that he had no thought of treachery. When Kark slept again he dreamed that Olaf had laid a golden ring about his neck, whereupon the earl remarked that the king will instead lay a red ring about Kark's neck if he is caught. Later on in the night Hakon was restless in his sleep and cried aloud. Kark was frightened and stabbed him and then carried his head to the king. When all the circumstances were related, the king ordered the thrall to be beheaded.[129]

The phrase "Ulle is dead" has no obvious meaning in this story and seems to have been borrowed from some tale in which it was significant.

We have now come to the end of the variants of our story of the death-message, that is, to the end of those in which the actors are conceived as having a human form. A

[128] Variant 242.
[129] Variant 227.

seemingly endless variety of creatures have participated in these stories: cobolds, vegetation-demons, house-haunting elves, dwarfs, changelings, the souls of the dead, and even a water-elf. No one of them appears to the exclusion of the others in an obviously earlier form of the story, and so far as one can tell by comparison, the folk seem indifferent to the nature of the actors, selecting the sort more favored by local tradition or the one suited to the form of the particular incident with which the death-message is to be combined. Certainly the story itself is not on the basis of this evidence an obscured vegetation-myth. Mannhardt's assumption that it is to be so interpreted rests upon a very insecure foundation, the fact that the creatures in the majority of the versions he cites are clearly vegetation-demons. He does not take sufficiently into account that, because of the incompleteness of his collections, he is dealing with a very specialized form of the story, distinguished by characteristic names and incidents and known only in southern Germany, Tyrol, and the adjoining parts of Switzerland. With more versions available for comparison it becomes apparent that the vegetation-demons in the story reflect the local preference for such creatures and not an inherent connection of the story with the forces of nature.

A large and important division of these tales has as actors cats instead of beings in human form, trolls, or demons. These stories about cats are characterized by a ferocity and gruesome imaginativeness unknown to the preceding tales, and the reactions of the feline hearer of the sad news exhibit a much greater variety of emotions. They are also interesting and important because they are widely disseminated, being current in Norway, Denmark, Germany, Bohemia, Brittany, England, and Ireland, and furthermore because they are demonstrably several centuries old, occurring in Irish story and history, German chronicles of the sixteenth century, English satirical pamphlets of the same period, and possibly in French historical tradition. This group is also significant because it affords confirmatory evidence of the non-dependence of the story on vegetation-demons.

The story may be told in the simplest conceivable way, as an incident in everyday domestic life, such as the following version from Haute Bretagne:

> Some one in the family circle happened to remark that the neighbor's cat had just been killed. The black cat before him on the hearth cried out, "Robert is dead!" to the astonishment and terror of all present, and with these words vanished up the chimney.[130]

The story was carried to Canada where it is told by the French-speaking population.[131] This Canadian version traces its descent from the group to which the preceding tale belongs, for both contain the phrase "Robert est mort!"[132] It differs, however, in that the cat is killed by the bearer of the news as he is endeavoring to make his way through a troop of cats across a bridge. This form of the story—the bringing of the message by the murderer— will be met with again in some very savage Celtic tales, and recalls the North German or Danish tales of the man who killed a dwarf. The Canadian tale is also linked with French sources by the fact that the scene is laid on a bridge, as in another example from the Pays du Dol (Ille-et-Vilaine). This last-named example[133] is peculiar, as it happens, because the narrator is directed to repeat the concluding formula rapidly and without variations; in other words, it has become a child's tale with a jingling, rhythmical close as follows:

> "Ta petit toutou [toi, petit trotteur] qui vas le petit trot, va-t-en

[130] Variant 237.
[131] Variant 243.
[132] See also a variant from Saint Cast, Haute Bretagne (Variant 230).
[133] Variant 236.

dire à Burline que Burlotte est morte. Burlotte est morte, fou, fou, fou."

The scene of the murder of the cat is also a bridge in a second tale[134] from Haute Bretagne: in this instance the man meets another—or perhaps the same—company of cats a few days later, and when he hurries back for his gun, he is delayed in returning by ditches and obstacles which are conjured up in his path. On the spot where the cats had stood he now sees priests celebrating a funeral. Surely this individual was subject to extraordinarily vivid hallucinations; possibly his second vision may be connected with the tales to be mentioned later in which the narrator sees not the murder but the funeral of a cat.

A close parallel to the first Breton story has been taken down in Canton Wallis (Switzerland):

A beautiful golden yellow cat was in the habit of visiting a family in the evening as they sat about the fire. It would come in with a dignified step, walk to the hearth, and seat itself in the warm ashes. One evening the family circle was discussing the news of the village and the death of one John N. was mentioned. Then the cat sprang from the ashes, crying, "What? John?" and ran off in long leaps, never to be seen again. The astonished household then guessed how all their secrets had become public.[135]

Here the reason for the cat's emotion is not clear; from the inapt concluding sentence one might almost suspect that it was chagrin at failing to know the gossip of the village. Gerhard, who seems to be unaware of the French parallels, terms this probably the most corrupted version of all. It leads Ranke, the author of a collection of German traditions with interpretative notes, to say in despair that it is "difficult or better impossible to search out the most primitive form of the 'death-message,' " in order to interpret it.[136]

[134] Variant 229.
[135] Variant 68.
[136] Gerhard, *Wiener Stud.*, XXXVII, 351, n. 4.

Another and seemingly whimsical modification, lacking in any suggestion of a death, is told in the Voigtland:

> A woman walking to Cronwitz saw a couple of cats dancing before her, and as she watched them, one called out, "When you come to Cronwitz, tell the parson's Rie, Ra, Ranze, she is to come to the dance." This meant nothing to the woman, but she told it at the parson's house and she had scarcely finished when the parson's cat jumped down from the shelf above the stove and disappeared forever.[137]

This story is accepted as a parallel by Henne-am-Rhyn and for that reason it is placed here. It is obviously an auditory hallucination, as is shown by the following parallels. Much the same sort of thing is told on the northern slope of the Brocken (Harz):

> At Hohenbruch (a quarry) many cats were once dancing. A man who was loading his wagon there heard a voice cry, "Tell your cat: if she does not come to this dance, it will cost her her tail." He did as he was told and never saw the animal again.[138]

The suspicion that this is a story of the witches' sabbath is confirmed by a tale from Klausthal on the opposite side of the mountain, where, as generally in Germany, it is believed that witches go to the Brocken on Walpurgis Eve in the shape of cats:

> Once at that time a woman and her daughter were returning from the village and had set down their heavy baskets at a cross-roads. While they were resting, countless cats passed and one of them addressed the elder woman, saying, "Tell Frau L. not to miss the dance." The message was delivered and Frau L. was seen to come out of the house in the form of a fat black cat and rush to the Brocken.[139]

Probably to be connected with this set of traditions is a story from Flemish Brabant which narrates how a man saw a company of cats dancing and singing:

> Poot aan poot!
> De(n) duivel is dood!

[137] Variant 62.
[138] Variant 38.
[139] Variant 39.

(Paw to paw!
The devil is dead!)[140]

A strange and unhappy alteration, showing the tale in a much degraded form, is printed as an Austrian tradition:

> When a man killed his tom-cat the younger cat left the house to call to the passing post-boy, asking him to enter an inn on his way and to invite the tom-cat there to the funeral, for old Mirermauer was dead. The astonished boy executed the commission. The murdered cat later appeared to the man whenever he went through a forest, as a man with a broad-brimmed hat and a long staff.[141]

There can be no question that we are here dealing with a corruption, for the characteristic name, Mirermauer, recurs in a Bohemian and a Silesian tale, as Mrnour and Meermauer, respectively.[142] These last mentioned tales are of the ordinary sort in which a cat is summoned to an assembly.

A somewhat similar story which preserves more nearly the original, is found in the *Zimmersche Chronik*, which describes life, manners, and events in the middle of the sixteenth century with an occasional jest or novella for good measure. This story is curious both because of its age and the manner in which the message is communicated. It is inserted in the chronicle as one told by Count Götfridt Wernher to explain his dislike of cats and his impatience at seeing them about when he was eating his meals—the last affords an interesting glimpse of contemporary manners:

> A nobleman with his servant was riding at night through a forest; he heard a loud burst of laughter in a tree and something inquired its meaning. It—what spoke is not clear—answered, "Should I not laugh since the sister-in-law of the Bishop of Brixen's cat is dead?" This

---

[140] Wolf, *Niederländische Sagen*, Leipzig, 1843, pp. 340–41, No. 246 and reprinted in de Cock and Teirlinck, *Brabantsch Sagenboek*, Ghent, 1909, I, 23–24, No. 15.

[141] Variant 118.

[142] Variants 113 and 13a; see the discussion in O. Kurtz, *Beiträge zur Erklärung des volkstümlichen Hexenglaubens in Schlesien*, Anklam, 1916, pp. 53 ff.

cat was, the historian explains, so spoiled that it sat on the table beside the bishop and ate the best morsels from the plate. The next day when the nobleman had arrived at the bishop's house he saw the bishop's favorite cat while at dinner and laughed. When, asked to explain his laughter, he told what had happened, the cat uttered a terrible cry, frightening all at the table, and jumped out the window. "What sort of a cat it was is readily to be seen."[143]

Among Evald Tang Kristensen's three score variants there are a few in which cats appear.[144] The first of them is typical of the rest:

In Snærild, Odder parish, a cat comes in every day and seats itself in the hearth, and as often as it is driven out, it returns. One day the farmer comes back from plowing and relates how he has heard the cry, "Svend Brat, tell your cat it should come at once, for Kurremurre is dead." The cat, which has listened to every word, springs up from the hearth, runs out, and is never seen again.

How such a story may originate is exemplified, in my opinion, by the immediately preceding tale[145] in Kristensen's collection, which, on account of its importance, I give here in a literal translation:

In Bjærggard in Nederby near Fur they heard one winter evening in the corner of the porcelain stove frequent rustling or muttering, which no one understood, until one day the door blew open, and some one whom they could not see came in and said aloud: "Tell Pils that Pjag is dead!" Whereupon the answer came from the corner of the stove, "Then we shall stay here no longer."

The following quaint experience[146] of a north German peasant, as related by Bartsch, reads like an adventure of a very credulous man with the voices of the night; while its folk-tale nature is demonstrated by the existence of a similar, although not exactly identical incident[147] in Oldenburg:

[143] Variant 79.
[144] Variants 209, 212–17, 218 (poodle).
[145] Variant 208.
[146] Variant 23.
[147] Variant 32.

An old farmer was going home in the evening when he saw a gray tom-cat walking across his field. "What are you doing here?" he asked. "Hm, what is the gray cat [fem.] doing at home?" the beast replied. The astonished man told all this at home, whereupon the cat came forth, saying, "Then, that is true!" and dashed through the window never to be seen again. Since then no cat on that farm has been an ordinary, everyday cat.

Fitzgerald has collected more than a score of Irish and Anglo-Irish versions, in some of which the names are chosen to imitate the mewing of cats. One of these, which he reports in full,[148] was taken down at Shannonbridge in 1882 and is particularly interesting because of the analogy of the cat's reply to that of the house-haunting forest-woman in a previously mentioned story.[149] It is as follows:

A large strange cat made itself at home in a farm-house. While it was sitting near the hearth, one of the women of the household asked jokingly, "Where do you come from?" "From Kill-gee-e-var (mewing)." And why have you been driven away?" "For having eaten the goslings." The frightened women drove it out of the house, and it said as it left, "If you had asked me more, I should have told you more."

Asbjörnsen's Norwegian version[150] differs a little from its Danish parallels, and suggests in some ways a dream-experience:

A wanderer, crossing the Dovrefjeld at Yule-time, stopped to spend the night in a hut. In it he found a huge black cat with shining eyes, and while he was thinking what he should do, one cat after another came in. He drove out a few of them, but gave up the task as unprofitable when he saw that two came in for each one he drove out. He waited for his postillion who had gone on to the next hut. Before long the boy returned and told the news that he had heard, that the vicar's wife in Lesje had broken her leg by falling on the steps and would scarcely

[148] Variant 136.
[149] See above p. 32.
[150] Variant 225.

live through the night. "What? Is great Pusje dead, then the rule belongs to me," said the black cat and went out in haste.

The transforming of a woman into a cat, as implied in this story, is a commonplace in witch-literature. The scene of the cats crowding in when the man tries to drive them out and their equally sudden disappearance recall the ineffectual efforts in dreams. Here, as in the majority of these stories about cats, joy at the prospect of coming into power fills the cat's mind. This situation contrasts very sharply with the almost universal sorrow with which the news is received by demons.

Our story[151] is told in Oldenburg with a slight difference which is quite in accord with the style of popular literature: the man is made to promise that the first words he will utter on entering the house will be, "Pusken, Peter is dod!" —and so on doing, his own cat replies, "If Peter is dead, then I am free!"

A fantastic modification[152] of the story was first put into print long ago by William Baldwin in a satiric pamphlet, *Beware the Cat* (ca. 1553), directed against the Church of Rome. This narrative, as comparison with other popular traditions proves, is not due to Baldwin's ingenuity, but is a folk-tale which seems to be known characteristically among the Celts in Ireland, Scotland, and Brittany. *Beware the Cat* is a framework story the inherent difficulties of which, says Brie,[153] are overcome with remarkable success, and from a technical point of view the work surpasses Chaucer's management of the genre as it appears in Baldwin's models, the *House of Fame* and the *Canterbury Tales*. (The estimate seems sufficiently high.) Baldwin and his friends are represented as disputing whether birds and ani-

---
[151] Variant 32.
[152] Variant 119.
[153] P. 317. The *House of Fame* is not a framework story.

mals have intelligence like men. The discussion has arisen from a dramatization of one of Aesop's fables. One individual, Streamer, defends the play even against the criticisms of its author, Baldwin, and gradually this figure comes to the fore, Baldwin disappears, and leaves Streamer to lead three days of discussion into which stories are worked with remarkable skill. The whole is dyed with hostility to Rome, which is satirized as the world of cats. On the first day two forms of our story are given, one localized in Staffordshire (see below) and the following thoroughly barbarous tale:

Patrick Apore and one of his followers made a foray on two lone houses, killed the inmates, and drove off the animals, a cow and a sheep, to a church where they intended to spend the night. There they built a fire, killed the sheep, and were making ready to eat it, when a cat came in, sat down beside them, and said, "Shane foel."[154] She ate one quarter of the sheep and continued to ask for more and to receive it until she had consumed the entire animal. "Like a cormorant," she asked for more and they, supposing her to be the Devil, gave her one and finally two more quarters of the cow. In the meantime they had set one quarter to cooking for themselves and, seeing that the beast's hunger was not satisfied, fled from the church. As they were riding away the servant saw the cat on the back of his master's horse and told him of it. He threw a dart which pierced it and killed it and thereupon a host of cats appeared. In the ensuing struggle the servant was killed and eaten while Patrick escaped with difficulty and rode home as fast as he could. He told his adventure to his wife in the presence of a six months old kitten. The "kittling" listened attentively to the narrative and at its conclusion started up and "said, 'Hast thou killed Grimalkin?' and, therewith, she plunged in his face, and, with her teeth, took him by the throat, and ere that she could be taken away she had strangled him."

Baldwin's story is, it seems, composed of two different incidents: our tale and the episode of the boy who is devoured by cats while fleeing with his father from them. At any rate the second incident has been related inde-

[154] Baldwin says that this means "Give me some meat"; but his spelling of the words is not accurate enough to permit exact identification of the original Irish forms.

pendently in Scotland and Ireland. J. G. Campbell prints the Scotch version as current folk-lore and conjectures that it may have been originally identical with a much earlier Irish story. The Scotch tale is as follows:

> Near Vaul in Tiree, a man riding home at night, with his son, a young boy, seated behind him, was met by a number of cats. The boy had his hands clasped round his father, and the man, pressing them to his sides, to make surer of the boy's hold, urged his horse to its speed. The cats sprang, and, fastening on the boy, literally devoured him. When the man reached home, with his horse at full gallop, he had only the boy's arms left.[154a]

The existence of this parallel to part of Baldwin's tale makes it probable that he was drawing on popular tradition for the whole; the voracious cat could, it is more than likely, be similarly paralleled.[155]

William Baldwin also tells a Staffordshire story[156] not very different from the Danish tales of Evald Tang Kristensen. It is significant chiefly because of its early date:

> A boy who showed a great affection for his cat at home was riding through Kankwood—a forest which exists today in Staffordshire—when a cat appeared before him out of the bushes, called him by name two or three times, and, while he was speechless with astonishment or fright, gave these orders: "Commend me unto Titton Tatton and to Pus thy Catton and tel her that Grimmalkin is dead." His own cat listened as he told this story to his wife and disappeared saying, "If Grimmalkin is dead, then farewell, mistress."

Savage variants of our story are yet known in Scotland and Ireland both as localized incidents and as floating, unattached episodes. Thus, for example, it is told to ex-

---

[154a] J. G. Campbell, *Witchcraft and Second Sight in the Highlands and Islands of Scotland*, p. 39.

[155] Compare for a start the *lon cráis* in the *Vision of MacConglinne*. Brie's suggestion (*Anglia*, XXXVII [1913], 332) that it is Baldwin's invention has little to commend it.

[156] Variant 120.

plain why members of a particular family would not tolerate a cat in the house:

Cameron of Doïni or Glenevis was out hunting, and killed a wild-cat. The animal, when expiring, asked him to tell, when he went home, that "the King of Cats (*Righ nan Cat*)" was dead, or according to others "the Key of Battle (*an Iuchair Chath*)," or "the streaked Brindled one (*a Bhrucail Bhreac*)." As he told his story, the little black kitten in the ash-hole bristled up and swelled, till it was as large as a dog. Cameron said, "You are swelling, cat." The cat answered, "My feathers and my swellings are growing bigger with the heat," and, springing at the chieftain's throat, killed him.[157]

No particular locality is assigned to the following, not entirely coherent tale, which seems to be a variant of the preceding one:

A hunter killed a wild-cat, and when he came home told his adventure. He said.
To-night has well prospered with us,
The big urchal-erchal has been slain.
A kitten that was listening rose and said, "Has Bald Entrails of the Cat been killed? If it were not the many nights I have got meat and milk in your family, I would have your long brindled weasand in my claws. Tell Streaked Foul-Face that Bladrum is dead," and saying this the kitten went away, and was never seen afterwards.[158]

Lady Wilde prints a variation of this story:

A man in a fit of passion cut off the head of his domestic cat and threw it into the fire. The head exclaimed in a fierce voice, "Go tell your wife that you have cut off the head of the King of Cats; but wait! I shall return and be avenged for this insult." A year later to the day, when the man was playing with a kitten, the little pet flew at his throat and bit him so that he died soon after.[159]

An analogous story from Haute Bretagne also fails to preserve the original outlines with complete faithfulness. When the farmer returned home he narrated his adventure:

[157] Variant 146.
[158] Variant 147.
[159] Variant 138.

He had seen cats about a cross and all but one of them fled on his nearer approach. The laggard crouched on the arms of the cross where he killed it. The others then drew near, crying, "Balthasar est mort!" On hearing this his own cat on the hearth rose and repeated the words, whereupon the farmer crushed its head with his shoe, saying, "And you, too!"[160]

A queer combination of our story with an Irish local tradition is particularly significant for us because it points very clearly to an origin in an auditory illusion. It is reported by Fitzgerald as follows:

> In a rock at Clogher there is an oracle which not only tells infallible truths, but which also will not tolerate a lie in its presence. A man named O Cathalain who had lost a mare had recourse to the oracle. He described his animal with foal, as he believed it to be. The oracle ordered him to go to Triucha to seek his mare without a foal. The irritated rock broke into two fragments, and a huge black cat appeared. O Cathalain killed the cat, which, before it died, commissioned him to inform his cats that he had killed the King Cat of Cruachan [the ancient place of resort of the kings of Connaught]. O Cathalain in due course repeated the message, and his cats killed him.[161]

This story deals with the materials of ancient Irish tradition: Cruachan was widely known as an entrance to the Other World, and O Cathalain may possibly owe his name to the famous King Cathal of Munster; but the actual antiquity of Fitzgerald's tale is open to question until its origin and narrator are shown. Supernatural cats are frequent in Irish tradition and myth; a "King Cat," possibly identical with the one here referred to, is said to dwell in the *sidh* or holy mount of Rathcroaghan in County Roscommon. There is another in the tumulus of Dowth, County Meath. The King Cat of Rathcroaghan appears to have been worshipped at a mount of eastern County

---

[160] Variant 231.

[161] Variant 130. For comment on this version I am indebted to Professors A. C. L. Brown, T. P. Cross, and F. N. Robinson.

Louth.[162] Fitzgerald remarks that the message, the portion with which we are more nearly concerned, is usually found in an independent form and that it occurs in "une longue et grave histoire irlandaise"—which I have not identified— in the following form:

> Tabhair scéal uaim a bhaile, Go Cronán Cilltealla, Cur mharbhaigh 'O Chealla Macanna Mór.
> (Tell the wheel of Kiltealla that O'Kelley has killed Macanna Mór ... or that O'Kelley has killed the King Cat of Ireland.)

Fitzgerald cites a further variation, which he calls "peu ordinaire," in which a man saw a funeral of the King of Cats, whom four cats, each holding a leg, were bearing to his tomb.[163] This variation is still current in Ireland; Lady Gregory prints a good example of it from County Galway in her latest book, *Visions and Beliefs in the West of Ireland*.[164] This instance is particularly interesting because of its resemblance to the more savage tales which have already been mentioned:

> A man going to the village to get something for his sick wife met a number of cats at a lonely spot in the road. They were carrying a young cat and "crying it." On his way back he met them again and one of them said, "Bid Lady Betty to come to the funeral or she'll be late." When he related his adventure at home his own cat looked up at first "affectionate-like," but when he told his message it jumped at his face and scraped it, she was "so mad that she wasn't told at once." It tore at the door and was let out.

This form of the story, which describes with more or less vividness the actual funeral, is frequently met with in Anglo-Irish, English, and Breton tradition,—and perhaps elsewhere. The picturesque and fanciful description in the following tale told by a Hereford squire about 1845 is prob-

---

[162] Westropp, "A Study of Folk-lore on the Coasts of Connacht, Ireland," *Folk-Lore*, XXXII (1921), 105–6.
[163] Variant 135.
[164] Variant 139.

ably quite independent of the literary version in Southey's *Doctor*:[165]

The younger of two young men who were on a hunting trip in the extreme north of Scotland went out to look for birds missing in the previous day's sport, while the elder remained in the hut. The younger man returned after a long delay and, after supper, told what had hindered his coming back. He had followed a light to an old tree, and looking down the hollow trunk, he seemed to be gazing into a church where a funeral was taking place. The ceremony was being celebrated by a company of cats; the coffin and the torches were borne by cats and in their midst was a coffin marked with a crown and a sceptre. At this the cat on the hearth rose, shrieking, "By Jove! Old Peter's dead and I'm King o' the Cats!" It rushed up the chimney and was seen no more.[166]

Quite as frequent in English tradition, however, is a less picturesque form exemplified by the following tale from Durham:

A farmer crossing a bridge was surprised to see a cat jump out and looking him full in the face, say:

Johnny Reed! Johnny Reed!
Tell Madam Momfort
That Mally Dixon's dead!

When this incident was reported at home the black cat behind the stove started up, saying, "Is she?" and disappeared forever.[167]

The most interesting use of our cat story is as a formula in certain Irish fairy-tales, in which connection Fitzgerald's tale about the King Cat of Cruachan is to be recalled. With significant differences the formula occurs three times in Larminie's *West Irish Folk Tales and Romances*, a collection noted for its fidelity to oral tradition. In "King Mananaun," for example, it is employed in the following form:

A champion engages to fight certain battles in behalf of others. He first kills an army of men and lies down among the dead to see what will

[165] Variant 124.
[166] Variant 129.
[167] Variant 131.

happen. Before long an old man and an old woman appear and begin to bring the men to life again. He rises and kills them all, but before dying the old woman puts him under bond to tell the Hag of the Church that he has killed the Hag of Slaughter and Slaughter himself. He goes on, informs the Hag of the Church of what he has done, and then kills her. She orders him to tell the Lamb of Luck that he has killed the Hag of Slaughter and Slaughter himself and the Hag of the Church. The Lamb fights in no gentle fashion, but is finally defeated and puts the champion under spells, "Tell the cat of Hoorebrikë that you have killed the Hag of Slaughter and Slaughter himself and the Lamb of Luck." He does so and has a terrific struggle with the cat in which both are killed. The champion is later resuscitated and the story goes on.[168] The whole recalls the cumulative tales, such as "Läuschen und Flöhchen"[169] and particularly those in which a child (or a mouse) dies by falling into a pot and the news of the death is repeated over and over again in an ever increasing series.[170] The resemblance of the Irish formula to the story of the announcement of the cat's death is slight, but in view of the example to be mentioned next, it is nevertheless significant. The champion of the Red Belt has an adventure very similar to that of Kaytuch in "King Mananaun"; he kills three hundred men, three hundred cats, the one legged hag, the Wether of Fuerish Fwee-erë, and then meets the King Cat of the Western Island, whom he also calls the "hideous hag." It is clear enough from the description of their duel that she is a cat (the confusion in gender—or sex—is not explained). The last injunction, that of the Wether, will suffice:

I lay on thee the spells of the art of the druid, to be feeble in strength as a woman in travail, in the camp and the battle, till thou goest to meet the King Cat of the Western Island. Tell him you have slain three hundred men, and three hundred cats, and the one legged hag, and the Wether of Fuerish Fwee-erë.[171]

[168] Variant 143.
[169] Grimm, No. 30; cf. Bolte and Polívka, I, 293–95.
[170] E.g., Wlislocki, *Märchen und Sagen der Bukowinaer und Siebenbürger Armenier*, Hamburg, 1891, p. 16, No. 40.
[171] Variant 144.

The formula ends as before with the death and resuscitation of the hero. The mention of the "King Cat of the Western Island" likens the formula to our story. Lastly, a corrupt and much condensed version of the formula occurs in the "Son of the King of Prussia." The text is so brief that it may be given entire:

"And he and the other people who were taking possession of his father's court began; and he and they spent three nights and three days killing one another, and on the third day he had killed and banished them all. But when he and the cat met, the cat killed him and he killed the cat; and his brother was going everywhere that he killed, and at last he found him and the cat dead."[172]

The part in which we are interested, the message, has disappeared entirely, and the entire formula has become so matter-of-course that no one would suspect what strange associates it has. Possibly, but I suggest it with some hesitation, the reason for the ferocious hostility of the cat, which is inexplicable or at best lamely explained, in some of the preceding tales may be due in some way to the story of the hag who was the King Cat of the Western Island. The fomula is useful, whatever may be thought of the interpretation, because it shows concretely how readily the cat and the demon (hag) could be transformed into each other, and it is therefore unnecessary to enter upon a disquisition concerning werwolves and their relation to the next considered tale to prove that point and thereby the identity of the two types of the story of the death-message.

Lastly, like the cry "Ulle is dead" in the *Olafssaga*, this story about the cat's end and its mysterious announcement loses its original meaning and comes to be used in other connections. Pluquet, for example, relates that near Bayeux *lubins*, a sort of ghostly werwolf, which visits churchyards in companies to dig out corpses, are led by a large black

[172] Variant 145.

lubin, which, as soon as men approach, cries out, "Robert est mort! Robert est mort!"[173] Thereupon the whole troop takes flight. Perhaps, as Uhland thinks,[174] this story is to be associated with Robert the Devil, but it is not difinitely connected with him by the narrator. It will be recalled that the cry "Robert is dead" has already occurred in several of these stories. But there are really no more substantial reasons for believing that the "Robert" of this tradition is the famous Robert of mediaeval story than the facts that both figures have the same name and that the modern tradition is current where that of the elder hero was once known. The identification is a bit of a modern collector's ingenuity, and there is nothing further in its favor. Pluquet's tale, although it is accepted without question by Gerhard, does not accord very well with the type under consideration, and it is readily explicable as an hallucination, an illusion based on misinterpretation of something seen or heard. Still more curious is the following children's rhyme, which seems to have been suggested by the use of our story as a nursery tale:

Nan, Nan, Dononré,	Nan, Nan, Théodore,
Pierre Quequette est monré;	Pierre Quequet est mort;
Il'a ieu peu du t'chat Margotia.[175]	Il a eu peur du chat Margotia,
	Que la souris l'emporte.

In another and hardly less widely disseminated group of these stories, which I accept as parallels only because Gerhard introduces one or two examples, the message conveys news of a fire and not of a death. Some Danish instances have already been casually mentioned and one more of them will illustrate how little this type of story differs from those that are already familiar:

[173] Variant 239.
[174] *Schriften*, III, 279; cf. p. 378.
[175] Variant 238.

A farmer passing by Hjulehöi (Hollow hill) noticed that it was raised on red pillars, that underneath there was music and dancing, and a splendid troll banquet. While he was watching the festivities, the merriment ceased, and a troll cried out, "Skotte is fallen into the fire." When he came home he related what he had seen and heard and a troll's voice from the cellar replied, "If Skotte has fallen into the fire, then I must be off." In his haste the troll left a large copper kettle.[176]

This, but for the message, is the story which has already been sufficiently illustrated, and the combination with the episodes of the hill raised upon pillars and of the beer-stealing dwarf has been remarked upon. The same form of the story, but without the strange metamorphosis of the hill and the incident of the forgotten vessel, is reported at least twice from Norway.[177] In one of these the dwarf makes answer, "Those are my children." This reply is, I am inclined to think, the original one, which has been somewhat obscured and modified in the Danish story.

The Irish form of the story resembles the Norwegian rather than the Danish tale, and this fact probably means that the Danish one has undergone some alteration. The Irish story, however, has a characteristic individuality: the news, as it is told in Connemara, is not a message of disaster but a cleverly planned stratagem to relieve one's self of unwelcome guests:

The mountain overlooking the beautiful Bay of Killary is called Mweelrea (The Bald King); and it is supposed to be sacred to the fairies, and a fairy's spinning wheel is somewhere concealed there. One day a woman who lived near the mountain was spinning in her cabin, when two old women carrying wheels came in. They began to spin, and their hostess, thinking they would like some refreshment, went out to get water for making tea. One of her neighbors saw her, and asked her what she was doing. "Faith, I'm going to give two dacint little women a cup of tea." "Shure, they're fairies," said the other. "What will I do, at all, at all?" "Tell them Mweelrea is on fire." So the owner of the

[176] Variant 171.
[177] Variants 223, 224.

cabin went back, crying, "Mweelrea is on fire." And the two women got up and ran out, leaving their wheels behind them.[178]

A wilder and much elaborated Irish story, which has striking continental parallels, contains a more intelligible response from the mysterious women and a queer description of their attempt to return:

> Two women in a cabin in a remote, mountainous district were disturbed by a knocking at the door. They made no answer, and a voice without asked, "Are you within, Feetwater?" "I am," was the reply from a pot of water in which the family had washed their feet before retiring, and an eel-like form rose from it and unbarred the door for several strangely dressed women to enter. While they were spinning one of the members of the household went out the open door and immediately rushed back, crying, "The mountain is on fire." The intruders ran out shrieking, "My husband and my children are burnt." When they had disappeared the women of the house took precautions against their return. The door was barred with the tongs, and the broom laid against it, an ember was thrown into the "Feet-water," a quill plucked from the speckled hen, the band removed from the spinning wheel, the carded flax placed under a weight, and the fire was made up. When the visitors came back, they called on "Feet-water," but the response now was, "No, I cannot, for there is a spark in me." All the other objects in turn declared themselves powerless to obey the commands, and the fairies departed with the imprecation, "May your tutor meet her reward."[179]

Two tales very similar to this longer Celtic narrative are reported as current in Lower Austria. They vary only in the details of the means used to keep out the unwanted stranger and in the fact that one injunction is forgotten, with the result that the woman in the house must spend the night holding one of the utensils back from opening the door.[180] Further examples of this story, which is known in Scotland, Ireland, Mecklenburg, Westphalia, Baden, and

---

[178] Variant 142.
[179] Variant 141.
[180] Blaas, "Volkstümliches aus Nieder-Oesterreich," *Germania*, XXIX (1884), 109–10, No. 19; Vernaleken, "Mythische Nachklänge," *ibid.*, pp. 411–2, No. 2. Blaas's references to Grimm's *Deutsche Mythologie* seem inapposite.

Swabia, need not perhaps be given, inasmuch as they will add little or nothing to the reader's notion of the tale.[181] We seem, moreover, to be getting away from the original story, or at least from the story with which we are more nearly concerned.

It is perhaps not necessary to say more than that fairies and changelings seem often to be much affected by news of a fire;[182] and consequently the Danish and Norwegian tales with which this section was introduced and in which also the relationship to the preceding types of tales was apparent enough may most conveniently be explained as a joining of our original story to an episode embodying the fear of these supernatural creatures for the flames. This group of tales contributes nothing to our understanding of the Pan tale and shows only the elaborate structures which can be built upon a simple incident, a procedure which by being illustrated once more may render some of the previous combinations and interpretations more plausible.

Here, perhaps, we may stop to examine the bearing of all these tales with their seemingly endless variations on the

[181] J. G. Campbell, *Superstitions of the Highlands and Islands of Scotland*, p. 75; W. Y. E. Wentz, *Fairy Faith in Celtic Countries*, 1910, p. 110 (Scotland); B. Hunt, *Folktales of Breffny*, p. 190; D. Fitzgerald, "Popular Tales of Ireland," *Revue celtique*, IV (1879), 182 ff.; Kuhn, "Westfälische Sagen und Gebräuche," *Germania* (ed. von der Hagen), IX (1850), 99; E. Meier, *Deutsche Sagen, Sitten und Gebräuche aus Schwaben*, Stuttgart, 1852, pp. 20–21, No. 11 (reprinted in Henne-am-Rhyn, *Die deutsche Volkssage*², p. 286, No. 435); Vonbun, *Sagen*, p. 16; Bartsch, *Sagen aus Mecklenburg*, I, 48, No. 68; Ralston, p. 201 ff.; Birlinger, "Volkstümliches," *Alemannia*, X(1882), 257, No. 5. Cf. Laistner, *Rätsel der Sphinx*, I, 210.

[182] See for example MacDougall and Calder, *Folk Tales and Fairy Lore*, Edinburgh, 1910, pp. 102–3, 188–9, and compare the nursery rhyme:
> Ladybug, Ladybug,
> Come fly away home,
> Your house is on fire,
> And your children all burned.

On this rhyme see Lady Martinengo-Cesaresco, *Essays in the Study of Folksongs* (Everyman ed.) p. 13; Kahlo, *Die Verse in den Sagen und Märchen*, p. 81; Blaas, "Der Marienkäfer in niederösterreichischen Kinderspruch," *Germania*, XIX (1874), 67–72; Wehrhan, *Kinderlied*, p. 23. It "has been pronounced a relic of Freya worship."

interpretation of Plutarch's account of Pan's death. Three tales, based on essentially the same incident, have been reviewed. The situation in them is to all intents and purposes the same: the announcement of a misfortune, characteristically news of a death or of a fire, to some not entirely "canny" creature and its effect upon the auditor. The first group, which has been examined at the greatest length and which possesses the most marked resemblances to the story of the death of Pan, is distinguished by the fact that in it the actors have human forms and often enter into relations of various sorts with men. Instances of this tale have been cited from all German-speaking lands, extending from the most southern, Carinthia and Tyrol, to the northernmost on the boundaries of Denmark and from Hesse and Baden in the west to Silesia and Bohemia in the east.[183] It has been taken down also further north: almost four score Danish variants are in print and there is evidence that it is not unknown in Norway. At least one French example has been remarked. And to one variant form we have noted an important and early parallel in the native Indian lore of South America. From the hastiest reading of a score of these tales it is abundantly apparent that there can be no possibility of deriving them from the Greek story. They are autochthonous products of an indeterminable age, possessing all the tokens of popular local tradition. Their origin will be considered later, but as a necessary preliminary to a discussion of that difficult problem it is important to review what we have learned about the tale and the actors therein from this collection of variants. Few of the instances of the first group, except the South American tradition, antedate the eighteenth century. One

---

[183] There are strangely enough no Dutch examples; Sepp's reference (*Altbayerischer Sagenschatz*, p. 597 to Wolf. 20) is wrong. I do not find the tale in Wolf. *Niederländische Sagen* nor in de Cock and Teirlinck, *Brabantsch Sagenboek*.

of the oldest examples, that told by Lady Charlotte Elizabeth in 1719, is on its face a corrupted version, implying the pre-existence of the usual form. The remaining instances, numbering considerably over a hundred, we owe to the industry of folk-lore collectors in the past century. Although these tales are therefore not remarkable for their age, they are very noteworthy for the variety of actors and scenes described. Dwarfs and house-haunting gnomes are favorites in northern Germany and Denmark, in central and southern Germany forest demons are preferred. Yet there are mentioned sporadically changelings (Carinthia, Tyrol, Denmark), a water-elf (Tyrol), and the souls of the dead (northern Germany and Denmark). Significant also are the combinations into which the tale enters. It is joined to the well-nigh universal incident of the demon which must depart when its name becomes known, although in this instance the juncture is not smooth enough to conceal the fact that the disclosure of the name seems, in comparison with the news of the death, an insufficient motive for the demon's flight. In some versions the story has attracted to itself the words spoken by a friendly house-elf on its departure: "If you had asked me concerning many things, I should have told you much." In the north of Germany and in Denmark it is combined with tales, which occur elsewhere independently, of unseen, thieving elves which leave vessels behind them in their haste and the union is ingenious, for here the death-message is made to explain the headlong flight. The story is also once brought into connection with the story of the cup stolen from the elves, but this version is possibly of literary origin and, although it may have been suggested by the former combination, it is much less clever. The inhabitants of Denmark and Schleswig-Holstein join the incident of the death message to an old mythical concept, the belief that the hills, conceived as the residences of the dead, open so that passers-by may look in. Here the combining of the two stories has occasioned their modification: the bearer of the message is himself the murderer of little Kind and he does not know that his announcement of the news is his death-warrant. Starting as this version does with the gnomes dancing in the hill, it is clear that we are dealing with actors who are really souls of the dead. There is current in Bavaria a single instance of the combination of the story of the death-message with the notion of an elf that milks cows, possibly a vegetation-demon. From a composite story told in Westphalia it is apparent that the actors are the dead: the death-message is attached to the incident of the souls ferried across the water (river or sea) to another land, a concept which is at least as old as the sixth century A. D. Here the union is looser and the death-message is not exactly in keeping with the notion of the transport of the dead, for their departure becomes a sort of flight, and the narrative seems to be modified to accord with those tales in which the demons flee before the advance of man. The combination must, however, be of some age, for it has attracted to itself a third and wholly independent story of a jealous wife. In Switzerland the joining of our story with that of the fleeing elves has also been made, and apparently without knowledge of the North German combinations. The combination arises from the nature of the stories and does not rest upon the ritual of a departing fertility-demon which is carrying away the prosperity of the land. Only in the extreme south, in Bavaria and Tyrol, is our story of the death-message united to the belief that the hero of the land sleeps in a mountain awaiting the call of his country. There is no reason for connecting the two incidents and the result is insignificant and meaningless. Also restricted to the south, to Tyrol, Bavaria and adjoining territories, is a very peculiar and easily recognized form in which the death-message is associated with creatures which are unmistakably vegetation-demons and which are distinguished by characteristic names: Rohrinda, Stutzamutza. The variations are manifold and indicate that the primitive archetype of this combination is of some considerable age. Indeed, there is no good reason for doubting that the occurrence of the characteristic names in the writings of a Swiss antiquarian of the sixteenth century is, although he does not tell the story, evidence of its existence at that time. If this be true, the story has maintained itself for three hundred years in Upper German territory. But no further significance attaches to this fact, and the age and abundant variations of this particular form do not entitle it to special consideration as the most nearly primitive type of the story. On the basis, at least, of the evidence thus far brought forward, the vegetation-demons which appear in this south German tale are not necessarily the original actors in the story, but are merely one of several competitors for that honor. In Saxony and Bohemia the death-message enters a new combination: it is united to two otherwise independent incidents, one of a dwarf's celebration in the room of a woman confined to her bed and another of three fortune-bringing talismans. This three-fold combination is interesting particularly because it is found in an early version, dating from the first quarter of the eighteenth century. The story as it is told in the island of Guernsey is more important for the purpose of arriving at its ultimate origin; it is joined, clumsily enough, with the incident of the midwife called to a dwarf-woman in childbed. The scene of the story, Le Roc du Coq Chantant, which is expressly mentioned in three independent versions, indicates pretty clearly the connection of the tale with auditory hallucinations. What significance attaches to the episode in the

Saga of Olaf Tryggvason is hard to say, possibly the story was in the narrator's mind. In any event, that episode alone forms a very shaky foundation for speculations about the god Ullr and for the construction of an airy castle of mythological speculations.

The second subdivision of these stories, namely those told of cats, forms, as is clear enough, a distinct group without any suggestion of the vegetation-demon. They are known throughout Europe and occur at a comparatively early time in widely separated places. They are told along with the anthropomorphic story in Denmark, Tyrol, and occasionally elsewhere in German-speaking regions, and are the only form in circulation on Celtic soil: in Ireland, Scotland, and Brittany. The earliest instances of the death-message belong to this type: English tales of 1550–1560 localized in Ireland and Staffordshire and one from Tyrol. Characteristic modifications which the simple theme has undergone are the associating of the story with the vision of a cat's funeral (Bohemia, Brittany, Scotland, Ireland), its adaptation to traditions about witches (Norway, Germany, Tyrol), and, most striking of all, the curious episode of the barbarous assault on the usually unoffending narrator (Ireland). This last episode is pretty clearly independent of the Dano-German tale of the farmer's murderer. Furthermore, the message of the King Cat's death is also worked into fairy-tales, and gets into some very strange connections with Irish mythology and folk-belief. The separation from the anthropomorphic tale seems fairly complete; the only trait in common is the parallel between the parting words of the cat in one tale and those of the demon: "If you had asked me, I should have told you more." But this, it has been shown, is the incorporation of an unattached episode into two otherwise independent stories. Except for this instance the story told of cats enters into combinations entirely different from those favored by the anthropomorphic tale. The cat story is also interesting as affording the nearest approach—neglecting one modern versification[184] of the other type—of the death-message to literature: the English satire is rated very high by its German critic, although literary historians have passed it by; the Tyrolese chronicle ranks among the best and most spirited of its period; "Monk" Lewis told the story to Shelley,[185] and, says Miss Repplier, Sir Walter Scott to Washington Irving.[186] The tale has just missed falling into the right hands or rather into the hands which were destined to give it final literary form.

A third group of tales which has been considered hastily tells of the fright caused by the announcement of a fire. A detailed examination of this form, which, although it is widely disseminated, is far from as abundant as the other two, does not promise to reward the effort. Possibly more than one distinct story is contained in the material before us. At any rate the Danish examples agree very well with the story of the death-message (for which merely the news of the fire is substituted without further change), and the others (Scotch, Irish, Swabian, Austrian) make the bringing of the message—which may be false—a stratagem to relieve the householder of unwelcome guests. Pretty clearly the latter stories represent an elaboration of simpler motives. It would be fruitless to speculate further on their origin and significance.

Many ways of explaining the origins of popular narratives and myths—for the two cannot always be separated—have been favored, and it is not out of place to comment on some of them in order to bring greater clearness into the

[184] Variant 30.
[185] Variant 5.
[186] Variant 123.

discussion. Once it was the fashion to see an Aryan myth in every tale. According to one's predilection for a certain manner of interpretation the story might tell the course of the sun through the heavens or contain in symbols the action of the forces of nature, but nowadays the glory of the sun-god is passed, and we need concern ourselves little with him. With the piling up of folklore materials for comparison other explanations have come into vogue. The origins of narrative are sought in the customs and experiences of primitive races, and psychology and anthropology are called into court. In recent discussions concerning the origin—not the dissemination—of tales two important modes of interpretation may, I think, be distinguished. The validity of either method rests wholly upon its success with the story in hand. The first, which will be exemplified by my interpretation of the Pan tale, declares that a given narrative takes its origin in some definite incident, that the narrative has an intelligible and far from mysterious basis in fact or life. Some märchen can be readily explained by comparison with experiences in dreams, so for instance Vom Fischer un syne Fru (Grimm, *Kinder- und Hausmärchen*, No. 19) and so also the folktale Shakespere utilized in the Induction to the *Taming of the Shrew* and the venerable exemplum of the King in the Bath, who, when he dipped his head beneath the surface of the water, lived a lifetime in the twinkling of an eye. Dr. Paull F. Baum has ventured the not unreasonable guess that the mediaeval tale of the young man married to a statue (Merimée's Venus of Ille) sprang from an actual incident of a man playfully fitting his ring on a statue's finger; fancy toyed with the notion, and the tale was made. One may similarly suppose that the saga of Orvar Odd, which tells how a prophecy that the hero should die by his favorite horse was fulfilled in spite of its death, has some foundation in fact: not improbably a man actually died from kicking a horse's skull. May one not guess that the legend of Don Juan owes its suggestion to some whimsical remark addressed to a skull?

Another line of attack on the mystery enveloping narrative origins finds support in primitive ritual, about which, it must be acknowledged, we know very little that is definite. Certain tales are declared to be more or less perfectly understood bits of ancient custom or ritual. Thus Miss Weston[187] would interpret the legend of the Holy Grail as the half-comprehended mysteries of the vegetation cult, cast into narrative form. Saintyves[188] sees in the story of Bluebeard and, indeed, in all stories of a forbidden chamber the reflection of the ceremony of initiation into primitive secret societies. The poems of the Elder Edda are based, we are told, on primitive dramatic fertility-rites.[189] Reinach holds that in the classical story of Salmoneus we have what was once a ritual to call up the storm clouds.[190] Without expressing an opinion on the merit of any of these efforts we may observe that Gerhard offers the same kind of explanation for the account of the death of Pan. Mannhardt had seen in it a story of vegetation-demons, and since he knew few instances in which the actors are not creatures of that sort, he did not feel the need for explanation resting on a broader foundation. Gerhard, however, is better aware of the multifarious actors in these stories and, therefore, offers an interpretation which he believes explains their existence: the Pan story is a bit of ritual associated with the cult of vegetation-demons. As the ritual was forgotten it has been misunderstood and made over into a folk-tale.

[187] *From Ritual to Romance.*
[188] *Revue de l'histoire des religions*, LXXXIII (1921), 1 ff.
[189] Bertha S. Phillpotts, *The Elder Edda and Ancient Scandinavian Drama*, 1920.
[190] *Rev. archeol.*, sér. IV, I (1903), 154 ff.

With the first method it is not difficult to show how the story of the death-message may have originated in an auditory hallucination, that is to say, in an incident likely to occur to anyone in any place. Whether the demonstration will be convincing will depend somewhat upon the reader's preconceptions. More convincing than any argumentation would be a reading of Kristensen's four score versions in which even the most enthusiastic can scarcely see a trace of a forgotten ritual.

Sir Walter Scott tells the following story in the notes to the *Lady of the Lake* (Note S):

> While two men were hobbling their horses for the night they heard a voice crying, "Tint! tint! tint!" One of them called out, "What deil has tint [lost] you? Come here." A misshapen creature appeared and so terrified them that they ran home. The creature followed them and arrived at the house as soon as they. It remained for some time and finally one evening a loud shrill voice called three times, "Gilpin Horner." It replied, "That is me, I must away," and disappeared.

The authenticity of the tale is confirmed, if need be, by the existence of a similar one in Cornish folk-lore:

> A farmer finds a little elf "apparently starving with cold and hunger," and takes it home with him. The bantling revives with kind treatment and becomes playful. After three or four days, while it is gamboling in the kitchen, a voice calls, "Colman Gray" three times from the farm-yard. It answers, "Ho! ho! ho! My daddy is come," flies through the key-hole and is heard of no more.[191]

What simpler form could the story have? Some fantastic sound in the night—with presumably an ascertainable physical basis—some voice calling a name, seemed to Gilpin Horner or to Colman Gray to summon him. Such airy voices that syllable men's names are familiar enough;

---

[191] T. Q. Couch, "Folklore of a Cornish Village," *Notes and Queries*, 1st Ser., xi, 397, 457, 497, xii, 37 (reprinted in *Choice Notes*, p. 73); Brand-Hazlitt, *Popular Antiquities*, III, 44. Miss Burne (*Shropshire Folk-Lore*, pp. 52-3) cites an unusual variation.

Marco Polo—and we may credit him in this particular if not in others—heard them in the Desert of Gobi, the shore-dweller hears the "call of the reef," the annual reciting of the names of those who have perished on the spot, the scene of the murder is still haunted by the echo of the crime and the voices of the actors, the ghost of the thieving farmer who has moved a landmark to his own advantage and to the disadvantage of his neighbor goes about asking where the stone should be placed, and so on ad infinitum. The most grandiose employment of such auditory illusions as these is the myth of the Wild Hunt, a fantastic chase of the dead across the night sky, and this shows a much higher degree of elaboration than do any of these simple tales.[192]

But, it may fairly be asked, does the simplicity of Scott's story represent an earlier, less elaborated form of the Pan tale or does that simplicity result from corruption, from the breaking-down of the tale? The intent to make the tale less supernatural and more human has affected it to a certain degree; Gilpin Horner is pretty clearly more human and less demonic than we might expect him to be. But beyond this possible change there is no reason to suspect Scott's tale and its parallels of alterations. It is clear from the structure of the story that, when the message is not imparted to any one as its bearer but is communicated directly to the individual concerned, there is no need to specify exactly what it is. A parallel to this situation may

---

[192] There are, furthermore, tales in which news of a death is mysteriously reported to a friend or acquaintance. These narratives are to be compared with the incidents in Gurney, Podmore, and Myers, *Phantasms of the Living*. Typical examples are Kuhn and Schwartz, *Norddeutsche Sagen*, p. 288, No. 322 and Grimm, *Deutsche Sagen*, No. 75. That old folk-lorist, Caesarius of Heisterbach, tells us how Priest Conrad of Rinkastle, who was on a pilgrimage to Palestine, heard from Etna the words: "In truth, Bruno is dead!" He noted the hour and later learned that the mesage was correct. See Caesarius, XII, 7 and Sepp, *Altbayerischer Sagenschatz*, p. 706.

be found in the preceding collections: the Lusatian forest-woman vanishes on hearing the cry "Deuto!" at the window. That cry or the calling of Gilpin Horner's name are such acousmata as have been described. The rationalistic explanation of the message heard by the wanderer in the forest or on the road as an auditory illusion is obviously hinted at in several of these stories, which have already been pointed out. The message is no more than a noise at the window, the air stirring in the forest trees, or the breeze whistling around a stone locally famed for its queer sounds. In general, the story is made more effective by indicating the nature of the news. The voice seems to utter a message—and the most moving message and the one most likely to be communicated in such a terrifying fashion and with such emphasis is a message of death. What else, the hearer might inquire, was the reason for calling the Lusatian woman away?

The enormous variety of names occurring in these tales makes it sufficiently obvious that etymologizing them will not throw light on the story's meaning, since it is impossible to arrive at the original form, or rather, at the original names. Clearly enough both whimsical and logical considerations determined the choice of the names: Fitzgerald observes that in many of his Anglo-Irish variants they are selected to imitate the mewing of cats, that rhyme and alliteration play their part. The impossibility of deducing the meaning of the story from the names is significant, for a substantial support of Mannhardt's theory that the story is told of vegetation-demons is his etymologizing of the names. The names may, to be sure, be useful in showing the distribution of certain forms of the story: Atis and Watis occur only in Danish and Low German variants, Find and Kind are confined to the same territory and even there to a particular form, the restriction of the names

Jochträger, Stutzamutza, and Hoch(Rauh)rinta to Upper German regions, and other less important groupings have been remarked upon—but more than this cannot be expected from the names, for there is no way of determining the priority of any set. Efforts to interpret the story by etymologizing rest upon faulty assumptions and are foredoomed to failure.

In every region where the story of this mysterious message has been told it has been readily adapted to the special variations characteristic of the local folk-belief. If, as in Mesopotamia, Syria, and Egypt, religious rites had made the folk familiar with the mortality of their divinities, then the story was accommodated to their religious observances in the manner we have seen. If, as in Greece, there was no cult of a dying god—Adonis was introduced from without—and the gods were believed to be immortal, then the story could find no ready resting-place among the myths. As a matter of fact, it came to be told of Pan, whose divinity was somewhat suspect, and even in his case the attachment, which may have been brought about by his obvious connection with the ever dying and reviving spirits of vegetation, appears to have been late. Pan it was who met Pheidippides near Tegea and through him encouraged the Athenians; the message which he sent to his followers seems to have been an auditory illusion of the sort we have been considering.[193] Of a similar nature also was the noise of a battle which the Methymneans, the captors of one of Pan's favorites, heard on a raid into the domain of Mytilene.[194] But it is not my intention to repeat Mannhardt's arguments for the identification of the story of Pan's death with the northern analogues. It was but natural to associate our story with the god who was supposed to utter the sudden

[193] Herod. VI. 105; Paus. II. 26. 4; Mannhardt, II, 132.
[194] Longus. 2. 26-8.

and terrifying sounds of the forest, sounds which as Apollodorus describes them, are incontestably auditory illusions:

> The mountains and gullies and all the caverns of the hills are full of echoes: as divers and strange sounds are made in the mountains by hunters and by animals tame and wild; and echoes imitative of these sounds are produced. Hence it is that often some people, not seeing the bodies of those who utter the sounds, but merely hearing the voice as it falls on the ear, say that Pan with the nymphs in the caves is calling to the accompaniment of flutes and pipes.[195]

If, as in the North, the story was for centuries told far and wide, it might be expected to enter into the greatest variety of combinations. The transformation and adaptation of the story to the spirit and substance of local tradition took place in southern Germany where the folk are particularly familiar with vegetation-demons resident in trees and forests and conceive them with unusual vividness. Such creatures are introduced into many stories taken down in that region. They are thought to visit the houses of men and to be called away by hearing the news of Rohrinde's death. But their appearance in our story is only a local peculiarity due to the South German predilection for these creatures, and their connection with it does not permit us to interpret the story as a myth of the dying spirits of the corn and the wild. In northern Germany where tradition delights in cobolds and elves the story is attached to them. The familiar tales about them—their thefts from the household stores, their weddings, their flight from the countryside, and the like—are joined, insofar as they lend themselves to combination, with our tale. It seems to have no close relations with the various North German vegetation-demons, unless cobolds are to be so considered. In England the story again shows a different facet, for it is now made to accord with the local belief and

[195] Quoted by Mannhardt, I, 131, n. 4.

interest in fairies, particularly with the notion of fairy funerals.
It is significant that the reconstruction of a primitive form from which several of the groups of the tale can be derived is impossible. No one species of demon can lay claim to the honor of being the first hero of the tale, so far as the available evidence goes. Some creatures to be sure are obviously late substitutions, as the water-elf and Eve's other children in the Tyrolese versions. This situation is not surprising when one recalls what has been said about the elves of Germanic myth:

No group of spirits is so hard to group as these, and perhaps their true nature lies in this very instability. They may be best characterized as a spiritualized race of men (not in origin, but as they are conceived), falling between the wholly material dwarfs and the immaterial spirits, and adapted to attract to themselves all sorts of fabulous tales and ghostly stories. They are not spirits of nature, as some have called them, but spirits *per se*, filling the natural world. The concept is instable and fits itself to the temper of the folk, so that the elves are scarcely to be distinguished now from the spirits of water, earth, forest, or air and now from dwarfs. Nowhere is the elf quite independent of the other creatures of the "lower mythology," and characteristically the elf is likely to become more and more like man.[196]

The fancy of the folk did not halt at these changing uses of the tale. Current along with the stories about demons, cobolds, and elves, we find similar ones about cats. When it was necessary, for the sake of the story, to assign the mysterious voice, which was undefined in Scott's tale, to some visible creature, demons and cats were apparently almost equally successful candidates for the honor.[197] But

[196] R. M. Meyer, *Altgermanische Religionsgeschichte*, Leipzig, 1910, pp. 115–18. This fluctuating notion of the Germanic elf is, as we have seen, admirably mirrored in the actors in the story of the death-message, and its tendency toward increasing anthropomorphization is discernible in more than one of the tales.

[197] We need not adopt Mannhardt's suggestion that, since Stutzamutza ("Stutzkatze") contains the word *cat*, all these felines are vegetation-demons. See also Mannhardt (II, 173) on the cat as vegetation-demon where some curious facts are collected and what has been said above (p. 48).

a further advantage appeared as soon as the division was made, the demons, being of human form and presumably possessing human emotions, could not be expected to act otherwise than as men on hearing the sad news. But cats, most unsympathetic of domestic animals, could act differently; sorrow over such a communication is not required of them and usually, as we have seen, the beast jumps out the window or up the chimney, rejoicing that now its chance to reign has come. The cat stories complete the picture; two contrasting emotions are possible when one hears news of a death, joy or sorrow, and in the tales we have read perhaps every shade of these two emotions has been hit on by the narrators. Rage, a third possibility, occurs both in the stories of demons and of cats.

The cat stories by exemplifying the emotion less likely to be found in man have from the start an uncanny air. The variations which are found in them are not considerable, but lead almost without exception into less and less human forms. The story becomes associated with supernatural oracles, acquires the flavor of witchcraft, and employs now and again the technique of dreams. Its more savage variants show an inexplicable and fantastic ferocity. When the stories are told as every-day events, without imaginative embellishments, they become flat and dull.

The episode in the Saga of Olaf Tryggvason illustrates one other way in which our tale may be degraded: the original significance of the message is forgotten and it becomes an omen of a different sort, bringing news of misfortune to one whose name is not mentioned in it. Why Ulle, possibly the little known Ullr, a doublet of Odin, lent his name to the tale would perhaps be intelligible if we knew more of the "lower mythology" of medieval Scandinavia. The question is now unanswerable—much as the reasons for the appearance of Pan in Plutarch's account or of Robert the

Devil, if it is really he, in the French story are not entirely clear. It is indeed not obvious that the Norse story actually belongs here, but I have accepted it because it appears in all lists of variants. One might perhaps interpret it as a narrative of an ominous dream with its fulfilment without insisting that the cry "Ulle is dead!" is more than a possible reminiscence of our tale.

In conclusion, Gerhard's explanation of the story must be briefly touched on. He regards the message as the annually reported news of the death of the vegetation-demon, a ceremony in the fertility ritual, and believes that this autumnal sorrow was paralleled by a rejoicing in the spring over his return to life.[198] The germ of this explanation was apparently a casual remark of Jacob Grimm's, who gathered a few instances of the death-message in a note and commented that this method of giving vent to sorrow over the death of a higher creature seemed to have existed from ancient times.[199]

Gradually, continues Gerhard, the understanding of this mythical ritual was lost and only the dark side, the message of death, was preserved, which, being unintelligible by itself, was misinterpreted by the folk in the ways we have seen. It may be "supposed," says Gerhard (p. 44), "that at bottom the vegetation-spirit which has fallen a prey to

[198] Mannhardt suggests no such combination of two contrasting motives, see, e.g., II, 208. Gerhard is very positive (p. 29) that Pan does not remain dead but comes to life. Need we fit every floating incident into a coherent life, a biography in human terms?

[199] He adds as parallels the Saxon "de gaue fra is nu al dot" and the Icelandic "nu eru dauðar allar disir," but it is not obvious that these phrases have anything to do with the story of the death-message. They could be better supported: for the first we have Grimm's remark that it is current in Saxony "with obvious reference to the maternal goddess" (Dea Mater) and for the second there is nothing substantial in the way of support; see Grimm, I, 333 where the proverbial phrase "ecki eru allar disir dauðar enn" (*Alfssaga*, c. xv) and the remark "yðr munu dauðar disir allar" (Rask, *Fornaldarsögur*, II, 47) are cited. From these Icelandic passages, found only in late, romantic sagas, it is a far cry to "nu eru dauðar allar disir," a lament for the death of a demon.

death is thought to be actually lingering in the form of a duplicate counterpart under the man's roof. It is the harvest-blessing on which the general prosperity depends and to which the individual house lays claim. We find here again the same primitive notion according to which the 'summer procession' must visit all the village houses in turn." This interpretation is confirmed, he holds, by the fact that the departure of the house-elf threatens, according to some of the narratives, to put an end to the prosperity it has brought. Nor are words of regret on its part lacking, as "If you had asked me much, I should have told you much." The departing Mao in a story from Italian Tyrol[200] throws a bit of food at the ceiling, saying, "So long as this clings, all will go well." The North German dwarf informs the householder, "You should put three crosses on the dough when you let it stand over night, then the dwarfs cannot take it." For this reason one still makes three crosses on one's dough when letting it stand over night. The vessel forgotten by the thieving elves is a pledge of good fortune. And finally, the notion of the good will of the parting demon is, he maintains, exemplified in the highly embellished Lusatian tale of the dwarf-wedding which is broken in upon by the death-message.

The passages which Gerhard cites as confirmatory of his interpretation are of rather uncertain value for that purpose. The sorrow of the departing elf and the destruction of the household's prosperity on its disappearance may be paralleled in other tales which have nothing to do with the matters in hand, and from which it becomes evident that we are dealing with an episode attachable to any departing figure, e.g., the widely disseminated incident of the helpful cobold who considers the gift of a new coat a sign of dismissal, and leaving in tears, takes with him the prosperity of the

[200] Variant 95.

farmstead.[201] The formula of the parting words of regret has been shown to be a commonplace which has found its way into our story by accretion. The story of the three crosses on the dough is obviously an etiological tale explanatory of a custom, and in such tales the connection between the custom and the explanation is often the most casual. The "forgotten jug" is similarly the excuse for attaching our story to the explanation of the origin of a queer bit of pottery, and it is frequent enough without the episode of the death-message. We have here as before only the combining of elements which may and do occur independently. And finally the fact that the story of the dwarf-wedding which is disturbed by the announcement of the message is composed of two (or more) quite distinct narratives is sufficiently obvious and has already been remarked. That the woman is confined to her bed after childbirth and that the dwarfs are celebrating a wedding are not facts to be employed to prove that the death-message is associated with fertility and increase, for these incidents are found elsewhere quite apart from the death-message, and the combination is late, fortuitous, and restricted in its distribution within very narrow limits (Bohemia and Silesia). Such tales as these cannot be employed to support the assertion that the original was a fragment of the ritual of a fertility-cult. It is quite clear that some, if not all, of these combinations belong to a late period in the story's history when its original meaning had been totally forgotten, and as a consequence such versions cannot be used to prove anything except that our story was just like any other in possessing the aptitude to enter freely into combinations. It is unnecessary and risky to deduce anything about the original significance of a story from a tale in which it is combined with another and quite distinct episode and in which both

[201] Abundant examples are collected by Feilberg, *Zs.d.V.f.Vk.*, VIII (1898), 145.

parts have been modified by forces which cannot now be estimated. And there is no reason for attempting anything so desperate when abundant instances of the story in an uncombined form lie ready to hand.

Gerhard's interpretation is given more succinctly in his second article, as follows:

> The Germanic parallels taught us that the capriform spirits of vegetation, the Pans and Satyrs, on the familiar announcement of the news by a human mouth, bewail the death of their chief, Pan, that same Pan, who, as the god of vegetation, originally died each year on the coming of winter to arise anew in the spring.[202] . . . A suggestive light is thrown on certain matters in literary history. That old Peloponnesian, prehistoric lament of the goat-demons must, shaped in dramatic form, have been the germ of tragedy as well as of the satyr drama.[203]

All that has been said indicates my unwillingness to accept that explanation. Vegetation-demons are usually recognizable as such and in Germanic folk-lore particularly have long retained a clearly marked individuality. Stories and rites employing the vegetation-demon in unmistakable guise—among them instances of the Pan story—are abundantly familiar in Germanic regions, and it is hard to believe that our tale rests on the obscured myth of such a creature. No more acceptable is it to suppose that it narrated an annual dying and regularly repeated wailing (*regelmässige Klage*), which, says Gerhard, is preserved in the feeling of vague mistrust exhibited by the dwarfs in the Saxon tale of the wedding, and that the foil, the tale

---

[202] He selects an unfortunate parallel (Variant 51) from the Germanic stock, see above p. 49. Since it belongs to the well-represented vegetation-demon type with the characteristic names Stutzi Mutzi and Jochträger, we can say positively from comparison with the score of closely parallel stories exhibiting the same names that this particular instance is a very much deteriorated version in which it is venturesome to look for a primitive trait. There is, so far as I can see, no cogent reason for thinking the dead demon in the German tales was originally a chief of any kind, although he has become one in the later forms.

[203] *Wiener Stud.*, XXXVII (1915), 347.

of the demon reviving with the vernal growth, was wholly lost. The folk's understanding of the true nature of the vegetation-demon did not disappear so completely, and to interpret the story in such a fashion is to miss its point entirely. Plutarch tells it as a unique instance, so strange that news of it stirred the curiosity of Tiberius. Had then its meaning and original content been also wholly lost to the classic world? If so, it is all the more strange that Gerhard should then venture to connect it with the origins of tragedy and in so doing assume the existence of a regular mourning of the vegetation-demon to be demonstrated by the Pan story. In every instance—exception need be made only for the Arabian parallels, which are explanatory of ritual—the point of the story is its unusualness, its bizarre atmosphere. The incident is an uncanny experience presented by the narrator as occurring but once and not the uncomprehended echo of regularly repeated annual wailings. Gerhard's explanation, furthermore, fails to take sufficiently into account the very curious cleaving of the variants into two large divisions, one in which the hero is a demon displaying human sorrow and another in which the hero is a cat exhibiting an inhuman joy or an unexplained ferocity. Nor does he pay due regard to the great variety of messages communicated, for it is out of the question to consider them all merely corruptions of a story which there is no good reason for expecting to break down. By failing to take into account all the variants he overlooks the barbarous Celtic tales in which the cat kills the bringer of the message; it is by no means obvious how these particular tales, which have every appearance of being unadulterated popular tradition, can be interpreted as myths of vegetation-demons. To defend the assertion that the story of the death-message is a ritualistic fragment it would be necessary to show that cats are in some way associated with the ritual and that this association was particularly favored on Celtic soil.

Furthermore, there is no occasion to indulge in wholly speculative reconstructions of a dramatic fertility ritual on the basis of non-dramatic materials, when just such a ritual, containing "Death" personified, is still performed. So far as I can discern, the present ritual, which has been often described, preserves fairly well the older ritual, the hypothetical basis of the Pan story. A brief sketch of the custom is therefore not out of place. At Mid-Lent and particularly on the fourth Sunday following (i.e., Laetare), the "Expulsion of Death (*Todaustragen*)" is celebrated in many German villages. The ceremony is usually coupled with the "Entrance of Summer (*Sommereinbringen*)." A straw puppet which has been carried about while the participants in the ceremony are singing is thrown into the water or burned on the fields of the villagers. As a second part of the rite, a staff or tree bedecked with ribbons, pretzels, or egg-shells is borne from house to house. "We have driven out Death, we have brought dear Summer back again," the participants cry and the bearers look for gifts of eggs, cakes, fruit, or money. Often only one of these ceremonies is performed or again both are combined into one. A special variation of the "Expulsion of Death" consists in throwing stones at a more or less perfectly made puppet. It is especially frequent to see young men, disguised as Summer and Winter, go from house to house, while they engage in dialogues which end in the flight of Winter.[204] Whether the custom of announcing the death of the master to the household animals and especially to the bees is a fragment of this ritual, as Gerhard conjectures, I leave undecided.[205]

[204] Cf. Sartori, *Sitte und Brauch*, III, 130–34 (with abundant references), from which I have condensed a summary of the customs.

[205] Richard M. Meyer was the first to bring that custom into connection with the story of the death-message, see *Altgermanische Religionsgeschichte*, 1910, p. 89, n. 4 and J. N. Sepp, *Altbayerischer Sagenschatz*, pp. 602 ff.; Gerhard, *Wiener Studien*, XXXVII (1915), 352. On the practice of announcing the house owner's death to the

The absence of any Greek or Balkan parallels to the story, which Plutarch localizes on the coast of Epirus, may seem strange, but, so far as I am aware, none has been taken down. The interpretations and discussions of the early fathers are of course wholly literary, based on Plutarch and not on any familiarity with local traditions of the Greek shores. The non-existence of any modern parallel saves us the task of examining that thorny question, the persistence of Greek myth in folk-tradition.[206] Collectors of folk-lore in this region have not taken down such insignificant tales as this and consequently its failure to appear will not serve as the basis for any speculations. The rocky shores of Epirus would occasion echoes. The topography of Epirus does not differ greatly from that of Tyrol, where we know the story enjoyed a remarkable popularity. If it originated in an hallucination, conditions seem to be sufficiently favorable for the production of the illusion in Greece. A more significant gap in the chain is the absence of early parallels to the story; the Arabian accounts are not wholly satisfactory, the incident in the Norse *Heimskringla* (or *Olafssaga Tryggvasonar*) is of dubious worth. There is thus a clear gap of considerably more than a thousand years, perhaps fifteen hundred, between Plutarch's narrative and the earliest instance of the modern story. The Irish instances, although one of them seems to be associated with old traditional figures and names, cannot be pushed very far back. Some French tales are, Uhland and others declare, attached to a mediaeval hero, to be sure, but it is not clear how ancient this attachment may be. No German

bees see an important article by Sartori, "Todansagen," *Zs. f. rheinische u. westfälische Volkskunde*, I (1904), 36–54 and also his *Sitte und Brauch*, I (Leipzig, 1910), 129, 144, 156; II, 118, 127, 132.

[206] The Cretan tale of Polites (see above, p. 57) seems to me a parallel version rather than a reminiscence of Plutarch's narrative. It came to hand when this article was in type.

example appears to antedate the story in Paul von Winckler's *Der Edelmann* (1696) and the corrupted version in the *Zimmersche Chronik* (1584). The oldest instances are those told of cats in Baldwin's satirical outburst of shortly after 1550, where the story is vouched for as occurring in Staffordshire and Ireland. No particular significance seems to attach to the fact that so many of these early versions are related of cats (William Baldwin, *Zimmersche Chronik*, and the French tales); it may be chance or it may be the heightening of a strange incident by narrating it of cats rather than of anthropomorphic demons. Of the very first importance, however, is the fact that these versions are early enough and widely enough disseminated to be wholly independent of one another. Few would suggest that a story from an English, anti-Catholic Reformation pamphlet of 1550 would be likely to appear in a widely divergent form a generation later in a local chronicle of Tyrol. The existence of a wide-spread tradition which reaches as far back as the early years of the sixteenth century is thus satisfactorily attested. Beyond this it is a long leap in the dark with only the shaky footing of the Norse story and the only slightly more substantial ground of the Arabian rites.

The precise explanation of Plutarch's narrative for which Professor Toy calls has not yet been given. Why the story of the death message was attached to Pan and the problems which this attachment raises in Greek mythology are still to be examined. Indeed, whether the northern tales are truly analogous to the Greek account is perhaps for the classical scholar to decide. The answer to that question, if it still needs to be answered, will not shake the truth of what has been arrived at here, viz., the voice of loud lament in these northern stories is an hallucination, an auditory illusion, and not a myth relating to the spirits of vegetation.

www.ingramcontent.com/pod-product-compliance
Lightning Source LLC
Chambersburg PA
CBHW071147090426
42736CB00012B/2258